I0579561

Kitchen Table Translation

Aster(ix) Journal

presents

Kitchen Table Translation

Summer 2017

Edited by
Madhu H. Kaza

BLUE SKETCH PRESS | PITTSBURGH

See page 202 for individual copyright information.

Published via Blue Sketch Press, Pittsburgh.
www.bluesketchpress.com

Kitchen Table Translation: An Aster(ix) Anthology / Aster(ix) Journal
Edited by Madhu H. Kaza—1st ed.

ISBN (print) 978-1-942547-06-8 (trade paperback)
1-942547-06-4 (ISBN-10)

Cover Design by Little Owl Creative. Cover image by Kolin Toney.
Copy-Edited by Joseph N. Welch III.

First Edition: July 2017

Printed in the United States of America
9 8 7 6 5 4 3 2 1

Thanks to Bill Martin and Sal Robinson, Co-Founders of The Bridge Series; Ken Chen and the Asian American Writers' Workshop; and Alex Zucker, Allison Markin Powell and Mary Ann Newman of the PEN Translation Committee, for their collaboration on the *Kitchen Table Translation* event series. Gratitude to Sitaramayya Ari, Gabrielle Civil, Rohan Kamicheril, Vivek Narayanan, Eléna Rivera, and Genya Turovskaya for the conversations that nurtured this issue. And thank you to Wah-Ming Chang.

Also a shout-out to a few translators and organizations—not included in this issue, but whose work inspires it. Check them out: Action Books: Johannes Göransson and Joyelle McSweeney; Ammiel Alcalay; Antena: Jen Hofer & John Pluecker; Sinan Antoon; Daniel Borzutsky, Kaima L. Glover, Jalada Africa, Sawako Nakayasu, Achy Obejas, Cristina Rivera Garza, Wangui Wa Goro, and Maged Zaher.

Aster(ix) Journal

www.asterixjournal.com

Aster(ix) is usually published 2–3 times a year in print with additional content online.

Funded in part by the Dietrich School of Arts and Sciences and the Department of English at University of Pittsburgh.

Contents

Editor's Note

Madhu H. Kaza

A few years ago the translator Bill Martin invited me to participate in The Bridge Series, which produces regular events in New York City focused on literary translation. Though I was grateful for the invitation, I balked. It brought to surface my anxieties around translation. Although I had published translations at that point, I did not feel comfortable talking about this work in the literary milieu of New York.

At some point I began to understand that my discomfort with translation was connected to the trauma of immigration. Something went quiet in me when I was brought to the U.S from India as a child. Although I assimilated and lost my accent, a vital part of me got stopped at the border. My inner life remained untranslated, its contours beyond what the receiving culture wanted to or could comprehend. As an immigrant child I felt an aura of illegitimacy about my claim to be an American. At times I lived with radical insecurity. As an adult, when I translated from Telugu, my first language (which I'd learned to read in college), I experienced a repetition of the loss I'd felt as a child. I not only worried about my own distance from the language but also wondered how the text I was translating would be received in the U.S., whether and on what terms it would belong. Translators often speak about the impossibility of their work, the untranslatability of particular words and texts from one language to another. What does it mean to be a translated self, I wondered? What does it mean to live with this untranslatability, this silence between languages within you?

Kitchen Table Translation extends from this personal experience to a greater curiosity about how immigrants, children of immigrants, or people who identify as part of a diaspora might bring a particular set of concerns to the task of translation distinct from the mainstream of literary translation in the United States. When the movement of texts (translation) is linked with the movement of bodies (migration), issues of language and culture necessarily collide with questions about politics, history, race and imperialism—the very contexts of migration and diaspora. Both in the *Kitchen Table Translation* events I curated and in this issue of *Aster(ix)*, I wanted to hear from writers and translators who could speak about personal, cultural and political dimensions of translation in relation to the technical and aesthetic aspects of the work.

The world of literary translation in the U.S. is largely white, and *Kitchen Table Translation* mostly features people of color. However, the primary impulse of this issue is not "diversity" or "inclusion"—terms which in the literary world can be impediments to rigorous and critical conversations about literary values. To be sure, *Kitchen Table Translation* invokes Kitchen Table Press, the feminist, women of color press founded by Barbara Smith and Audre Lorde together with a collective of radical women of color. Instead of seeking admission into the existing literary institutions, they forged new possibilities and built new structures, creating the first woman of color press in the United States. Their groundbreaking work changed the terrain of (deterritorialized) American literature. It is a meaningful connection to me that whomever is included in its pages, *Aster(ix)* is a journal run by women of color.

People of color, then, are not a bonus to be added to the regularly scheduled literary programming. I see *Kitchen Table Translation*'s contributors not as a representative group and not in terms of a congratulatory diversity, but in terms of difference. They do not necessarily share a particular approach to translation or the same literary taste. Nor do they all equally identify as immigrant or diasporic subjects. But I'm interested in the particular intelligence of each of these various writers and how they open up problems and possibilities for literary translation.

When it is even acknowledged, much of literary translation in the U.S., especially of prose, is appraised in terms of fluency, which often coincides with ideas of accessibility and seamlessness. A fluent translation avoids literalism and awkwardness (translatese); the wrinkles that would remind us that it is translation are ironed out. There is an emphasis on the translator's mastery of language and an artfully inconspicuous technique. Whereas in most parts of the world—particularly in post-colonial contexts—translation is recognized as inherently political, discussions of literary translation in the U.S. emphasize formal concerns with a light attention to cultural variance.

How might we think through these values? What are questions we might ask? There are the questions of what gets translated and why. And then how? If fidelity and submission to the original are marks of a good translation, how might errant, disobedient translation serve us? If fluency and domestication are prized, what might a translation that reminds us of the text's foreignness offer? Translation can function politically in a range of ways. Translation theorist Lawrence Venuti argues that the Anglo-American emphasis on fluency "enacts an ethnocentric violence." In this sense, fluency can be compatible with multicultural and cosmopolitan celebrations of translation that nevertheless do not seek to interrogate the dominant culture or its existing norms, and which are only superficially interested in difference. Translation can also perform subtle acts of critical resistance by introducing texts into the English language that speak from marginalized voices and values, or through modes of translation that do not seek to erase the otherness of the text.

Kitchen Table Translation seeks to make space for the fact that translation can be an intimate act, and many of us use our translation skills in non-professional as well as professional capacities. Some of us, when we translate, call on our family (rather than colleagues) to help us with challenging passages or words. Some second generation, diasporic and indigenous writers who speak (or partly speak) an ancestral language at home might find the discourse of mastery fraught, especially when access to a language has been lost through historical violence and dislocation. And some of us experience translation all the time in our bodies, names, homes, movements and daily lives even if we are not translating from one text to another.

Personal experiences of otherness can potentially lend creative and critical charge to the work of translation. In *Kitchen Table Translation*, Sony Coráñez Bolton's essay offers one possibility of a decolonizing translation practice that draws from Gloria Anzaldúa's queer, borderland, Chicana feminism and critiques the ideal of mastery from the perspective of disability studies. Don Mee Choi presents translation as one response to U.S. imperialism and the pain of migration. Lina Mounzer invokes American hegemony in her recognition that the English language is not neutral in relation to Arab worlds.

Writers like Zohra Saed and Gabrielle Civil connect translation directly to family history; In Saed's account of her work with Langston Hughes' archive, translation is a genealogical archeology that must accommodate the fissures and silences of history. Civil's performance score not only amplifies translation errors but also uses moments of failure to contest the strictures of translation in the academy.

Amy Sara Carroll's poems are part of the Transborder Immigrant Tool, a project which provides navigational and safety assistance for migrants crossing the desert between Mexico and the United States through an app for flip phones. The poems, translated collaboratively and published under a Creative Commons license, engage a translation ecology in which authorial autonomy is de-stabilized and translation itself becomes a continual crossing by many different translators across a landscape.

Eiko Otake, who is primarily known as a movement artist (half of the duo, Eiko & Koma), has translated a book that stands apart from much of contemporary Japanese literature in translation: Nagasaki survivor Kyoko Hayashi's travelogue of her pilgrimage to the White Sands nuclear test site in New Mexico. Hayashi's book, a work of profound witnessing and empathy, evokes questions about war and peace, suffering and the environment. It's a book that Eiko urgently felt needed to be read by American readers, especially in the aftermath of 9/11. In her introduction to the book-length translation, Eiko reflects not only on her choice of text, but also her approach to the ethics of translation: "I decided . . . that I should risk awkwardness in English. Hayashi's voice came from her body, and it should stay connected to her body. I did not want Hayashi's work to be translated into such smooth English that it could be read as if an American woman were writing." Dagmawi Woubshet similarly maintains the poignant jaggedness of the fledgling style of the children, Ethiopian AIDS orphans, whose letters to their dead parents he translated. These translations draw our attention to the subjectivity of individuals (whom he calls the disprized) whom we mostly only encounter in the U.S in reductive, generalized terms of African otherness.

In a lecture given at the American University in Cairo, the Iraqi born writer and translator, Sinan Antoon spoke movingly of translation as an act of mourning. Psychotherapist, poet and translator, Genya Turovskaya, whose family fled the Soviet Union when she was a child, has described her return to the Russian language through translation as the repairing of a wound. In *Kitchen Table Translation*, multiple, overlapping and sometimes conflicting notions of translation live together: translation is conceived of as a mediation between personal, family and political history; a summoning of spirits, a transplantation—of seeds, of organs; a return from light into darkness (where migration is the movement from darkness to light, though these terms do not carry their conventional values); a gesture of solidarity, a flight of shadows, an act of decolonization, an entrance into afterlife, a bodily transfiguration, the border crossings of language, an experience of inter-subjectivity, the closest possible reading.

For me, with all its predicaments, all the violence it may carry on its back, translation is an act of hospitality. Hospitality, conceived not as charity, not as condescension or even merely tolerance. A hospitality that recognizes both the dignity and the difference of the other. In this model, translation is not about assimilation—of the other language or the other body. The impossibility of any particular translation is not a difficulty to be overcome, just as the difference of an immigrant, a refugee, or anyone deemed other is not a difference to be overcome, but rather greeted with care. Translation can be a practice of hospitality that acknowledges that the host, too, will have to be changed by the encounter. We may unravel and have to remake ourselves with others. This is not a simple task that can be celebrated in the usual glib ways, but it is beautiful and worthwhile. In the words of Youmna Chlala:

> First, we had to learn each other's languages.
> This was the longest, most loving trial.
>
> Then we undid our own.

In Search of a Word

Rosamond S. King

Benn
Ńaar
Ńett
Ńeent
Juroom
Juroom benn

when you have language but no one
to speak it with
eventually the words
fall on the ground
unremembered

Juroom ńaar
Juroom ńett
Juroom ńeent
Fukk
Fukk ak benn
Right?
And now this is all:
Nanga def hello, how are you?

and then hands up
stopping code
switching *I don't know*
anymore degg olof tutti rek
Fukk ak ñaar
Fukk ak ñett
Fukk ak ñeent
Fukk ak juroom
Fukk ak juroom benn
I will not ask you to count
what got left behind.

Do you remember December?
When home was snow surrounding fireplace
almost all your children together and
cozy it was cozy—?
Fukk ak juroom ñaar
Fukk ak juroom ñett
Fukk ak juroom ñeent
Ñaar fukk
My well-rehearsed speech, the book
about parenting such a child, the phone
number for PFLAG, the passage
from a novel, a mother telling a daughter she knows
without saying she knows
Ñaar fukk ak benn
Ñaar fukk ak ñaar
Ñaar fukk ak ñett
Ñaar fukk ak ñeent

Lesbian was only said once, but love
three or four times. Do you remember
December? Maybe should have
waited for summer, daylight
at least, so it wouldn't all
seem so foreign. *This was one*
of the things of this country
from which we were trying
to save you. Yes
your grammar
was perfect.

Ñaar fukk ak juroom
There is not
even a word in
our language
for this.
Ñaar fukk ak juroom benn
Do you want this sentence back?
I give it to you now clean, polished
from years of repetition. Without
malice—just it is yours and
I don't want it anymore.
Ñett fukk
There are words for this
in our language.
doom ju jigéen
Yaay Mama
doom ju góor
Papa Baay
Sissy

Auntie
Cousin
Uncle
Ñaar fukk ak juroom ñett
Oumar
Bejamin
Juroom ñeent fukk ak juroom ñeent
Rosamond
Olufunke
Teemeer ak benn
In our language there are words for
nob
bëgg
love

The Paper Camera
(excerpt)

Youmna Chlala

> To translate . . . would mean engaging an electrical circuit in his brain, bypassing his heart.
>
> —LUC SANTE

Mannerisms in language
slashes above A's, marks below long Y's
when reading Arabic these are not printed
just understood
this is how you knew that you would leave before I did

Variations between
                        letter and sound
                        Kha
                        is released
from the back of the throat
force and muscle   spit and saliva and tongue against teeth.
The difference is a minute tongue induced difference

When they ask where you come from, tell them:
Don't believe in origins. Authenticity died with Colonialism.

Find a worn Arabic phrase book, practice saying *Ghorba.*
a kind of home, outside of language

Ghorba: Gha is a fricative sound.

Even if your mouth is closed (you are a mouthpiece)

Where are we in the legacy of crusaders?

(make sense of it all in translation)

First, we had to learn each other's languages.
This was the longest, most loving trial.

Then we undid our own.

French, all is a run on.
Arabic, codes, departure
encounter in transition
if authority then authentic, the I returns.

Collective, pronoun as mispronunciation
of proper name, translation demands
greater knowledge of the self, a kind of ort.

Ornamentation, a third dimension
for example, bolts, thunder, underwater god
holds the silver screws in place.

Narration, voice again from below
instructions arrive in apparitions
the motivation is in the tongues.

Fur meaning close to cypress
but not quite that, rows of
narrow trunks that would not
allow anything between them

a pink light on the needles of pines
softness in hundreds of small pricks
space accounted for by trees

m+m++

mattar (rain) + *mattar* (airport)
sound the same, if mispronounced

What is the matter?
ma—fee—shee (nothing-there-is)

"Mama, will they take pictures of my whole body?"
"No honey, just the heart."

A city is only as good as its satellite dishes
and Yo Te Amo is a big big word

I tell you as a seal moves slowly towards us
slick mass of muscle and a cartoon smile
on the beach where buildings recede
behind chlorinated pools

we are famished, eat sambousek and tabouli
you tear the lettuce leaves, give me the cœur
say, she who is heart will fight.

Langston Hughes in Turkestan

Zohra Saed

> How did I, a poor American Negro, get way down south in the Union of Socialist Soviet Republics—way down in Tashkent, Bokhara, Merv, Samarkand—almost to the Indian border, almost to Western China? I sat in the courtyard of Tamerlane's tomb and wondered, "Am I dreaming?" I looked at the camel caravans starting out into the Kizil Kum, saying to myself, "Is this me, way over here in oldest Asia?"
>
> —LANGSTON HUGHES

Langston Hughes wrote this passage in a handwritten draft of his essay "USA to USSR," and I often returned to it while researching his archives at both the Schomburg Center for Research in Black Culture in Harlem and the Beinecke Rare Books and Manuscripts Library at Yale University. I can easily reverse the path of Hughes' journey and ask: "How did I, a poor graduate student of Uzbek roots and Afghan birth, get *here* to Harlem?" And just as Hughes felt elated as he sat by the tomb of Amir Timur, so I felt the same, standing over Hughes' ashes interred beneath a floor medallion in the foyer of the Schomburg.

As I sifted through Hughes' handwritten notes, clippings, and photos of his journey to Central Asia, I achieved two things: I traced the travels of an African American poet to an unfamiliar place, and I found threads of my own family history, which begins in the very places that Langston Hughes visited and wrote about: Tashkent, Samarkand, and Bukhara.

Mir Fauziljan, my great-uncle, was thirty years old sometime after 1921 and before 1925 in Tashkent, Uzbekistan. He was a descendant of an aristocratic family and served as governor in Soviet Tashkent. During the day he worked for the Soviet mission while, at night, he supported the counterrevolutionary movement of Turkestani nationalists, the *basmachi*. He fed the *basmachi* the locations of weaponry, goods, and other relevant information. *Basmachi* means the "overtakers." In the Turkic languages, to bas (pronounced more like the English word "boss"), means to press down on; and machi is the one doing this. The *basmachi* are "ones who press down," to claim, or otherwise "take possession." The Bolsheviks used the term *basmachestvo* to mean "marauders" or "thieves" in reference to how the *basmachi* dressed, covering their faces, working at night, and using stolen weaponry. The roots of an uprising that broke out in 1918, when some 25,000 Turkestani people were killed, were seeded in the anti-conscription movement several years earlier, in which Central Asian peoples refused to serve the Russian Empire in the First World War.

The legend I was raised on was that the *basmachi* wrapped half of their faces in disguise and worked on stealth missions at night. Women were part of the rebellion, and dressed in *paranji*, full veil that covered their body and faces. Growing up, my grandfather witnessed a group of women—wives, mothers, grandmothers—rolling out the famous Turkestani carpets that they wove by hand on the new train tracks that connected Central Asia to Russia. The men were on horseback ready for ambush. The carpets worked to derail a train filled with potatoes. Since potatoes are not native to Central Asia, they were transported in from Russia as a cheap food source for the military. The women took the food supply while the men stole the weapons. These kinds of attacks required inside knowledge from other *basmachi* working in the Soviet government. *Basmachi* members were also White Russians, elites from the former Imperial Czarist regime, who supported nationalist movements in an attempt to destabilize the Soviet government.

Being a double agent was one of the worst crimes in Turkestan in the 1920s. As Edward Allworth wrote:

> At the Sixteenth Congress of the All-Union Communist Party in Moscow (1930), where Stalin ordered campaigns against "local nationalism" and "great-power chauvinism," the Party was instructed to fight for complete exposure and eradication of ikkiyuzlamachilik (dvurushnichestovo) (double dealing), which was described as the new tactic of anti-Communist groups by which they ostensibly bowed to the Party but actually continued to resist it.

Double-dealing as a nationalist counter-revolutionary strategy had been in use as far back as 1921.

Accusations of being *ikkiyuzlamachilik*, a double-agent (literally meaning "two-facedness" in Turkestani), and working for the *basmachi* were taken quite seriously and those accused were quickly killed. Mir Fauziljan's identity as a *basmachi* had been made known to Soviet officials. A fellow *basmachi*, a White Russian named Gorgy, notified him that the military was on their way to find him. Before being captured, he fled on horseback to Kazakhstan with another *basmachi*, hoping to make it to China.

The Soviet soldiers rounded up the remaining members of Mir Fauziljan's family, young and old, including my great grandparents, my great uncles and aunts, and took them to their *hovli*, courtyard, where they were all shot. The elaborate home of the Mir family, once symbolizing the harmonious merging of former Turkestan aristocrats with the Soviet government, became a gruesome reminder of Soviet power. The fear of being implicated along with this *ikkiyuzlamachilik* family was so great that no one would come out to bury the victims, and their bodies were left out to instill further terror and fear in the *basmachi*. In the midst of this massacre, Mir Fauziljan's half-brother, a three-month old baby, Mir Hussein, was the lone survivor. His mother had shielded him with her body. Another younger brother, Mir Kaamiljan, seventeen years old at the time, was en route from Moscow, where he had been attending school. This frightened teenage brother of Mir Fauziljan, who stood at the gates of his family home, now an open gravesite, would become my grandfather. Kaamiljan rescued his infant brother from his stepmother's arms. The remaining *basmachi* helped Kaamiljan flee on horseback, also through Kazakhstan.

Meanwhile, Mir Fauziljan reached Ili, China, through Kazakhstan. Ili was known as Almaliq, for its small sweet apples. Kublai Khan had a penchant for the apples there and so he had favored this area during his reign in the thirteenth century. It is a place where multiple languages are spoken, even now. Renamed as Yining Province, bordering Kazakhstan, there are still Russian signs on stores and Turkic languages are spoken among other languages. In Ili, the Soviet soldiers caught my great-uncle. He had shaved off his hair and had worn clothing to fit in with the villagers, but his height, at six feet, gave him away.

To make his trial official, Soviet soldiers planted a red flag with a hammer and sickle in the grass in front of the home where he had taken refuge. Even though they were on Chinese land, the soldiers were brazen enough to act as if in Soviet territory. In the makeshift trial—on land that was only temporarily colonized—Mir Fauziljan was sentenced to death and publicly hanged. The soldiers then reclaimed their flag and went back across the border to Kazakhstan. He must have known that he did not have much time because he had given a friend, another *basmachi*, a photo of himself in China, and a letter to take to his younger brother, my grandfather, Kaamiljan. The friend had hid in a nearby home and watched the "trial" and the lynching. Once the soldiers were long gone, he buried Mir Fauziljan and read the letter.

The letter urged my grandfather to flee to India. It never reached him, though he did eventually make it to India after much hardship—first in China, then on a caravan trip over the Himalayas to enter British India. According to a note scribbled in the family's Holy Quran, also used to record marriage dates, births, and new homes, Kaamiljan invested in a new home in Bombay in 1933. He prospered in India, putting himself and his brother through dental school in Hong Kong, in case the factories he had built were no longer viable. The Hindu-Muslim riots during the partition of India-Pakistan in 1947 did indeed destroy the factories and, soon after, he fled with his wife to Afghanistan where my father was born. Had my father been born a few months earlier, he'd have been Indian. They settled in Jalalabad, Afghanistan, where my grandfather, Kaamiljan, and great-uncle, Mir Hussein, served as the first dentists.

By a miracle of timing and chance, the letter reached my father a generation later when he was in Saudi Arabia during the 1970s oil-boom where he, also trained as a dentist, had taken us. There my father met political refugees from Turkestan who had fled to the cities of Taif and Mecca. The tightknit communities comprised of 1930s refugees (now Saudi citizens) were referred to as "Bukhari." It was here, when my father was at a dinner party, that an elderly survivor approached him and asked if he was the son of Kaamiljan. Once assured of my father's lineage, he recounted the story of Mir Fauziljan's death. This was the same man who had witnessed my great-uncle's lynching at the hands of the Soviets who had illegally held court in China. By this time both Mir Kaamiljan and Mir Hussein had passed away. My grandfather lived his life longing for his brother, whom he believed had perished trying to cross the Himalayas. A week after my father met him, the elderly survivor passed away. He was well into his nineties when he passed these things on to my father. This devotion to my great-uncle's memory is how I know this family history and how we have this photo of Mir Fauziljan:

This compelling story of my own family remained with me as I conducted my research. It is significant that Hughes' trip to Turkestan came at a crucial moment in Central Asian and Russian history, just at the fall of the *basmachi* and the Turkestan Nationalist movement (1917–1932), and just prior to the infamous Stalinist purges (1937–1938). The last of the Turkestan nationalists were brought to trial circa 1932,* the same year as Hughes' trip, and the word "basmachi" appears in his

* This is how a diaspora of Central Asians was created in Afghanistan, Saudi Arabia, South Asia, Turkey and the US. The term Turkestan is now used mainly to refer to the North Western regions. In Saudi Arabia, refugees from Turkestan were among the few who became citizens. Last names like Turkestani, Kashgari, Bukhari, are the legacy they have maintained, but not many preserved the language. In the United States, New Jersey claims the first Turkestan American Association. It was through this route that we came to the US and ended up in an area of Brooklyn filled with Crimean Tatars, Turks, Kazakhs and Uzbeks.

notes.

Hughes makes note of an older Turkic language, Chagatay, that connected the majority of Turkestan. It is the language I speak at home. In some cases, exilic consciousness tends to preserve languages and customs as if time stopped at the moment of migration. In my family's personal time capsule, we continue to speak in this rather antiquated Uzbek. This is not just us, but a diaspora of Turkestani people who fled Central Asia in that time period.

This family gift of language, tenaciously preserved in exile, proved invaluable in helping me translate the notes on the margins of documents and the poems of Karim Ahmedi in the Hughes' archive, and allowed me to give names to the faces of the people Hughes befriended. In the midst of this treasure of photos, letters, poems and translations, this journey has been an intensely personal process for me, unfolding a chain of significance from Hughes's journey in Central Asia to the long-lost traditions of Turkestani poets and, finally to me, the great-niece of the *basmachi*.

Karim Ahmedi: Poem for Langston Hughes on His Arrival to Uzbekistan

Karim Ahmedi was a poet Langston Hughes had contact with, and identifying him required sleuthing: I came across him initially in multiple copies of one particular photo of a handsome young man's profile taken by Hughes. He is dressed in a three-piece suit. On the back is a personal note written in Latinized Uzbek: Respected Friend Hughes Langston, a small memento." Karim Ahmedii 20/1 -33. After identifying the name, I traced Ahmedi to another photo taken on a snowy street in Tashkent. He was dressed in a traditional Uzbek chapan, the multi-jewel-colored robe, the one Hamid Karzai made famous when he was President of Afghanistan. He stands with Hughes in front of a giant wheel. Hughes is in a wool coat and hat. Both poets are smiling and the note on the back simply says: "Hughes with Uzbek poet."

Though not part of the 1933 group portrait of Central Asian and Russian poets taken in Tashkent, Uzbekistan, Ahmedi is one of the Uzbek poets Hughes photographed several times and with whom he was photographed at a meeting with Central Asian writers. I found his ten page poem, written in the old Chagatay or Turkestani script, at the Beinecke, filed under the name "Karen Akmadi, Arabic." Hughes had a rough English translation, filed in a separate folder under "Karen Ahmadi." Had I not been looking directly for Karim Ahmedi, the file of translations would have been overlooked. The translation Hughes kept on file doesn't capture the nuances of the original and, if we look at the two versions side by side, a number of questions emerge.

Many Uzbek poets of the 1920s and 1930s wrote coded poetry. According to Allworth, "A special vocabulary for designating Russians was used in some compositions by nationalist poets. Muz Ayiq (polar bear), zalim (tyrant), vakhshi (barbarian), and many others could be understood in this historical and literary context as allusions to Soviet Russians in Central Asia." If we read the poem in this light, Ahmedi refers to slavery and lynching but uses coded terms. Could he have been trying to communicate with Hughes? Was he connecting the African American experience with that of the Turkestani people under Soviet rule? It isn't clear. But choosing to write in the old Chagatay script instead of the Latinized script, the use of coded terms, and the inconsistency of the poem's style, raises the question. Hughes would not have been open to such connections, and the translation he has on file, along with his designation at the end of it, "Dour Soviet No. 3," seems to confirm this. Perhaps Hughes' positive impression of the acceptance of African Americans in the Soviet Union stood in such stark contrast to segregated America that he was unable to perceive the parallel sense of oppression Ahmedi may have been trying to convey. While we may never know the answers, finding these poems has at least allowed us to ask the questions.

Ahmedi's version of this poem is difficult to read. The Arabic handwriting is unsteady, many of the words are misspelled, and probably reflects the official change in script perhaps in mid education. Arabic script, like cursive, is written continuously, but here the letters are not always strung together, making the poem a challenge to decipher because the meaning becomes fluid. Does this letter connect with this one and create this word, or does it lean to this other word and connect to make a different word. Translating this poem has been like deciphering something written in sand, a slant of light changes and the word changes. Perhaps this is intentional. The poem itself shifts in mood and allegiances. The poem is divided into quatrains, a curious move since the Soviets discouraged archaic Turko-Persian styles in contemporary writing. Though it begins in the flowery, lyrical format of a love poem, it doesn't maintain the form or style, veering into something much more sloganeering towards the end. Here, for the first time, is an excerpt, translated by my father. Directly following is the version that Hughes had on file, along with his designation at the end of it, "Dour Soviet No. 3."

Poem for Langston Hughes on His Arrival to Uzbekistan

Crossing many oceans, you've come
Leaving your family behind.
I saw you and I felt wrapped in the
curls of your hair.
The black and white of you,
a protective eye talisman,
entered my poor home.
When I looked in your beautiful eyes,
I loved you. In front of your glowing
face,
your words came like stars and now
you must hold my words.
I am powerless in the face of the
Komsomol.
I am hiding . . . The Negroes are a
sacred race . . .
low is anyone who calls them
barbarians [vakhshi] . . .
our tongues are folded away,
we have many novels, poems that are
woven in tears.

Translated by Abdulsamad Saed

37

Listen to me, my Dear Langston

To L.H. on his arrival to Uzbekistan
I greet your arrival!
The hero man—hey you! Who came
Across the ocean!
The lion who conquered the waves of the sea.
I am bound to you as tightly as the curls of your hair.
And when I saw your eyes
I loved you!
Welcome you, the poor son of the West!
When my eyes look into your
Lively laughing eyes I see the suppression
Of your people.
But when I see your smiling face
I raise my fist against the West!
Why? Because in your face there are winds of
Cold bitter days.
Their aim is to take you by the throat
To oppress you! The devils!

Found Translation from Hughes Archive

whisper (the index of suns)

Gabrielle Civil

"*whisper* (the index of suns)," an original performance art work, embodied my experience translating Jacqueline Beaugé-Rosier's neglected 1966 masterpiece *A vol d'ombre*, what I came to call *At shadow flight*. The performance showcased my early translations of Beaugé-Rosier's text (marked by an asterisk here in the text). It also linked literary translation to my cultural translation as a diaspora subject and daughter of a Haitian immigrant (and revealed family secrets).

The work wallows in errors—from literal French/English mistakes, to the call-outs of my mistakes by others, to the actual misnaming of my mother's birthplace. (My mother would like everyone to know: she was born in *Gadsden*, Alabama, not Selma.) This is part of what makes the text interesting today. To err, to wander, is part of the translator's path, her guilt and revelation.

*

whisper (the index of suns)

My Room of Memory

Every object touched, activated, and remembered is already here—from rum and sugar to ribbon and chalk. Mounds of plastic multi-colored flowers. A frilly, hot pink negligee and a chalkboard hanging in the space. Tall, glass candles offer images of saints. When the stage lights dim, the candles keep a steady glow.

The black woman translator arrives.
She will assume many roles: the teacher, the daughter, the diva.
No matter what, they are all her. Wearing a black slip, she pulls a piece of chalk from the bucket of sugar cane and a small lit candle from its side.

She draws a line from the right side of the cane all the way off the stage. For a moment, she disappears. She returns to the cane, picks up another candle and draws another line to the opposite side of the stage.

She speaks. I was born in Detroit.
She sets the candle down and walks the line back to the sugar cane.
She picks up another lit candle, draws a line from the back of the bucket of sugar cane to the back wall.

My mother was born in Selma, Alabama.

She picks up a final candle and draws a line to the front of the stage.

My father was born in Port-au-Prince, Haiti.

The Story of the Two Phones

There were two phones in our house.
Rrrring! Rrrring!
Guess which one that was.
The phone upstairs, well
that was what you might call the public phone.
It was the phone that when you gave out your number
you gave out your number for.
The phone downstairs, well
that was something altogether different.
That phone was connected to a secret answering machine.
People would leave messages. Secrets. Whispers.
Wanting to be healed.

The daughter gets down on her knees and draws the vèvè for Legba.

The sound of the needle hitting a record. The music begins, an old time Haitian song, a kind of French calypso. She places her hands on her hips, kicks her heel, kicks out her hip and shimmies across the stage. The chalkboard awaits. The music stops.

Audience Translation

The music turns into the beep of an answering machine. Someone leaves a secret message. The black woman translator has never heard this message before and it changes each night. As it plays, with her piece of chalk, she begins to translate the words she hears from English into French. After the message ends, she continues to translate the memories this message evokes.

(Message: Sunday. 12 AM. If I'm fundamentally a good person, I'm honest, I'm compassionate, I'm generous, I live within my means, why do I live with so much shame. Bye.)

(The black woman translator writes: a e i o u . je suis bonne, pourquoi est-ce que j'ai assez de problèmes => je suis généreuse, honnête, => je sais encore je lis => que je suis merveilleuse mais seigneur j'ai besoin d'aide)

She draws two stars and a line as if for Legba on the chalkboard.
She stands for a moment, feels the channel of other voices within her.

She holds onto the chalkboard for a moment.
She turns and begins to speak.

Jacqueline Beaugé-Rosier Lesson

> *A vol d'ombre* is the second volume of poems by Jacqueline Beaugé, an elementary school teacher, born in Jacmel, Haiti in 1932. Published in 1966, at the height of Papa Doc's terror, *A vol d'ombre* is fashioned as one long poem, broken into sixteen unnumbered parts.

As she speaks, she walks toward the mound of flowers. She stands before it. Her body slowly sinks to the ground, until she is sitting on her knees.

> Published in the indigenist "Hougénikon" series by L'imprimerie Serge Gaston, the text is influenced by both negritude and surrealism. Rhapsodic and lamentic, it promotes a vision of Haitian 'protest poetry' as personal, displaced, ecstatic and written in standard French. Overall, it is a poem of love.

At these last lines, we see only her face above the mound of flowers.

Context / Explanation

She stands, pulls out a black scarf printed with flowers.
She lays it on her head and ties it like a kerchief with the knot at the back.
She pulls a pile of three books up from behind the flowers, and sets them on her head, the biggest one at the top.
She moves across the stage, shifting her hips, her hands holding the books to her head.
Music as if from a zippy French film from the 60s plays softly in the background as well as the translation of her speech.
The English translations of this text are also projected as subtitles on the back wall.

(Live speech) *(Voice over)*

Je suis née à Detroit.
I was born in Detroit, MI.
Ma mère est née à Selma, Alabama.
My mother was born in Selma, Alabama.

Mon père est né à Port-au-Prince, Haïti.
My father was born in Port-au-Prince, Haiti.

Le temps a passé. Time passed.

À 1996, j'ai suivi un cours de traduction
à l'université de New York.
In 1996, I took a translation practicum at New York University.

Mon projet final était la traduction
du texte <<A vol d’ombre>> du poète
Jacqueline Beaugé.

My final project was a translation of
Jacqueline Beaugé’s *A vol d’ombre.*

Mon professeur et moi,
nous ne marchions pas du tout.

My teacher and I did not see eye to eye.

At the end of this speech, she takes the books from her head and drops them to the floor next to the candle in a huff. She pulls off her kerchief, bends down, picks up the matches and lights the candle. She then picks up the piece of chalk which becomes a cigarette. She becomes her translation teacher. Her voice is deep, unmistakably masculine and pompous. As she speaks she walks over to a red square of sequined fabric spread out on the stage. At key points, she brandishes her chalk cigarette, puffs and blows.

The Story of the Teacher (w/Chalk)

Gabrielle—

A very ambitious undertaking indeed. You’ve chosen an extremely difficult task—largely because Beaugé’s French is so distant from—and recalcitrant to—English, especially her surrealist tendency toward the “surrealist cognitive” (x de y de z . . .). This said, I nonetheless think that your versions are marred by too many elementary misreadings of the original French. I spent a long time going through your translations line-by-line—so please study my corrections carefully. I did so because you are clearly engaged by

> Beaugé, so it's absolutely crucial that you avoid simple mistakes . . . As for the overall tone and rhythm: I agree with your decision to open up and ventilate the poem through stanza breaks within the lines. The main thing you have to catch is the religious tone of these poems—very akin to the spiritual ecstasies of St. Theresa—a female voice, bride of Christ, addressing her mystical lover (Abidhou). For this reason alone, "vertige" should be rendered as ecstasy (which she also uses) or trance (which she also uses). "Overwhelming," I think, just doesn't make it . . .

At the end of the speech, she sets the chalk down on the red fabric and walks away. She goes to her black shoe box tape recorder and presses play. She puts on her old-fashioned, black, high heeled shoes. The sound of her voice reading the original French text plays.

Negligée Pin-Ups

She pulls down Jacqueline's hot pink negligée and lays it on the chalk line that cuts through the room of memory. She gets down on her knees, flexes her body and lays her body down on her side on top of it, her face to the back wall. A recorded voice of her speaking her story of her origin in French plays (Je suis née à Detroit, Ma mere est née à Selma, Alabama, etc.) Projected lines from the poem appear on the wall behind her. Some of the language falls onto the chalkboard, still scrawled with her translation of the secret message before. On the wall, we see:

> *If only you could live for my désert
> If only I could be mirrored in your warbling song
> *Que tu vives pour mon desert*
> *Que je memire dans ton ramage*

inharmonique

She turns her body toward the audience, elbow bent, head propped on one hand, knees bent, one high heeled ankle over a knee.

*la nuit rouge d'hallucinations
Mon vers étouffe du mal de gorge
Que nous vivions les cheveux emmêlés de luttes
O my voice veiled in sweat
night vision-red
at the throat

She sits up, back arched, head tilted back.

*If only we could live like hair
Tangled up in fights

She turns, lifts her body up, casts her gaze down to the side.

*I cannot possibly be alone
Crossing the straits of my memory
The pure waters of innocence
Abidhou my love, your heart hurts me so

Duet with Jacqueline's Spirit

She gets up, picks up the negligee and begins to dance with it to Wyclef's "Jaspora."
She flourishes the negligee, moves with it in the space, turns off the tape recorder and begins to speak.

problems of phrase fragments and line formation
problems of demonstrative and personal pronouns
problems of definite and indefinite articles
moments of only extrapolated connection

She repeats the above lines and the dance changes. It is no longer a union with Jacqueline's spirit, but a consideration of her own mistakes. She drops the negligee, continuing to repeat the mantra.

problems of phrase fragments and line formation
problems of demonstrative and personal pronouns
problems of definite and indefinite articles
moments of only extrapolated connection

Possession

She speaks these words in a stream, moves to stand on the red square of sequined fabric.

problemsofphrasefragmentsandlineformationproblemsofdemonstrativeandpers onal
pronouns problems of definite and indefinite articles moments of only extra
polatedconnectionproblemsofphrasefragmentsandlineformationproblemsofdemonstrati
veandpersonalpronounsproblemsofdefiniteandindefinitearticlesmomentsofonlyextrapo
latedconnectionproblemsofphrasefragmentsandlineformationproblemsofdemonstrativeandp
ersonalpronounsproblemsofdefiniteandindefinitearticlesmomentsofonlyextrapolatedconnection[illegible]
[illegible]
[illegible]

As she speaks, her arms start to propel the words out of her body. The words become a kind of trance, moving through her body and becoming a shrill moan or howl. At the end, she stomps on the professor's chalk. She gets down on her knees and in quiet, spreads the chalk remains across the red fabric.

She anoints her cheeks with the ground remains and walks away.

Rum Tea with Jacqueline

She walks over to the small table with flowers and tea cups. She sits for a moment on the stool, picks up a piece of chalk, takes off her high heels and draws the a vèvè for Damballah, two snakes. Faint drums and piano play. She returns to the stool, picks up the bottle of rum, pours a libation on the floor and takes a swig. She lights the small candle. Lights dim as she holds the glass of light in her hands. The lights come up and she sets the candle down, turns over the upside-down cup, pours rum in it and sets it down on the vèvè with its saucers.

*I have followed innumerable films
Of crucifixions with you
My nights vaccinated by you.

She pours rum in the two cups.

My heart star shattered for you
On parallel lines of night and day

And tonight the dream of your smile takes shape
Your smile that doesn't stop from turning
To the weather cock of visions.

She lifts up the red tin and offers her guest powdered sugar.

Ah these steps those shouts of my blood revolted
Against life as a means of escape

Her guest must have refused the powdered sugar.
The black woman hostess sets down the tin.

Stretch out   dream

She picks up both cups of rum tea.

If your stupidity scratches to the crackles of stars

She leans forward to offer a cup to her guest.

My arteries break the last records of patience

She exchanges her hands, offers the other cup.

And all that concerns the span of time

She pulls back both cups, holds them both before her chest.

For your wisdom and its ecstasy
I loved you.

She sets both cups down on the table.

Between these silences and space
The index of suns would beg us
To store up doubt
Before the explosion of our thunderbolt hearts

Time has not wronged these emerald poems
Carved in the thickets of our embrace

My childhood my joy my sweat
My weariness
All the music played on bridges of mirage
The rages of birds of innocence

She picks up the red tin and begins to walk back to red sequined cloth where she sprinkles powdered sugar into the chalk.

All the calls laid low at the foot of the cross
The lapping of my muddled memories
And my shadow on the look-out for wind
Cut out my colorless desires

She wipes the sugar onto her cheeks.

In burning verses of daily talk.

She gets down on her knees, face to the back wall. She presses,
dabs the mixture of sugar and chalk on each of her shoulder blades.
She blows out the candle and secretly places a coiled red ribbon in her mouth.

The Notion of Silence

She stands and begins to speak these lines from her dissertation while slowly pulling the red string of ribbon from her mouth until it becomes a long, wet line. Behind her key words from her text appear projected on the wall.

The notion of silence as a part of Haitian women's literary expression resonates with their social and political situation.

> Discussing the marginalization of Haitian women within their own culture, Chancy suggests that "from this marginalization emerges a sense of women's culture that defines itself through *its silencing*." Perhaps it is fitting that Beaugé considers her poem as a silence, a madness and sense, born in shadow and destined for mummification. This image is prescient as *A vol d'ombre*, one of the most magnificent, original and revelatory works of Haitian literature itself has been silence for years.

At the end of the speech, she reaches down and pulls up the curled black boa and stuffs it into her underpants.

The Streets of Silence

With her hands, she beckons the audience, then places her hands before her as if she is reading a book. A voice-over of her voice reading the poem in French plays in the background.

> *My very own legend my delight my whore
> My age dedicates the bees of its pain
> Streets dance masks dance
> And Sunday is cold
> When you and I dream vigorous dances
> Turning like a nightmare on the streets
> Of silence
>
> The streets of silence have filled the house
> And I haven't the fire to receive the hope
> That they have brought to my interior doubt

The streets of silence have raided my room
And I haven't a dream to offer your arms
The oasis of your dreams

The streets of silence have slept on my breasts
And I haven't the fire to refuse the love
Which you bring to overwhelm me

The streets of silence have embraced my fear
And I scarcely have the time to steal from life
The small amount of faith that it refuses me

The streets of silence have closed my lips
And all I have left are your eyes of light
To enclose my shadow

The streets of silence have broken my desire
And tonight I no longer have this quiet space
Where our hearts speak
In the immense desert of your absence

Undress

She walks to the back of the room and with her hand tries to wipe off the translation of the secret message from the chalkboard with her hand. It remains. She takes off her slip, stands in strapless bra and underpants. She wipes off the chalkboard with the slip. As she does this, she speaks, the original French floating up in lines behind her. The sound of her voice in the background speaking these lines in French floats through the air.

*Then my heart nailed through
My hands sticky from his moist wings
My body your impassive lips
Follow the flow of the wind
Whose tongue can no longer be still

Superimposition

She drops the chalk stained-black slip. The light turns red.
She pulls the red ball gown from the chair and slips, zips her body into it.
She pulls out a mirror and strokes the chalk, sugar from her face.

*And yet your steps walk in my steps
Tonight when I'm sick of dreaming
Tonight when my tears can flow no more

Still my life endures
And I hear you who comes into my night
No the silence of moons
Would have perfected the unpublished poem
I listen to the prelude at your shoulder

My love
Enter as you will into my silence
And close the door

I love and demand nothing of you

The streets, the tears, the cares the home
I do not have the time to think of them

So sad the night without your steps in my steps
So sad the night without your eyes
Where my face becomes deformed

And here I am disturbed again by the suaveness
Of this dream offered to my woman's heart
I listen to the silence slacken off
My silence speaks to the trees on the path

She walks over to the red sequined cloth, blows out the candle, shuts the sugar tin, folds the cloth in the square and sets everything on top of it.

Across from my room the trees have cried
Gold unaltered from our hands
O damn it all without seasons O life that is not
Detached at all from my insides
Cursed by the fire of your groans

She walks over to the stool and table, blows out the candle.

Mumble to my heart your strange confidences
Show me your smile
Let my silence forgive you
for not creating its eyes
The poem of this life

She straightens the tea cups and places them on the stool.

For your weakness
I would like to be
The source of the tree

Where you find yourself again.

She slides the calla lilies and straw flowers into the stool. Breaks down the small table and sets it against the newly laden stool. She walks to the back wall and blows out all the candles.

The Secret Room

She pulls up a large bouquet of flowers. She twirls, her full red skirt wide in the air.
She walks to the audience, tells her story while offering flowers to people there.

I was born in Detroit, MI.
My mother was born in Selma, AL.
My father was born in Port-au-Prince, Haiti.
There was a secret room in our house.
A place none of us talked about.

On the back wall, a projection appears with these words:

les bougies	*les saints*
les messages	*un répondeur*
le poudre	*les os*
le vertige	*la craie*
le cataclysme	

We lived under the spell of this room.
It was like the smell of burnt lard and cooking.
It was everywhere. It was unspeakable.
One day, I decided to go down and find out

what was in that secret room. And what did I find
but pictures of saints and chalk and dirt and silk
flowers and a phone and an answering machine
and a pile of books. And I reached for those books
and I opened one up and inside there were pictures
and inscriptions and words in French. Et maintenant
chaque bouquin en français est ce bouquin. And now
every book in French is that book.

Diva Lullaby

The black woman translator walks to the sequined square and picks up a piece of chalk. She gets down on her knees and, with the bouquet in her arms, draws a vèvè to Erzulie. She hums as she draws, a song she heard as a child. She taps the chalk in percussion to her tune. When the vèvè is complete, she stands and sings, translating the words in French into this occasion.

Bon soir mère, madame fais do do
Bon soir mère, madame fais do do
Bon soir mère, madame fais do do
Bon soir mère, madame fais do do

She repeats the song more softly, laying the flowers down on the vèvè.

Benediction

She stands with what is left of the bouquet in arms, near the vèvè of Erzulie now strewn with flowers. Behind her these words project.

*To you one would have believed my love
I offer to you these chants
To you one would have called my soul
I leave to you my soul
We lived ever in the repercussions of love
The roads resound the memory.

She sets the flowers down next to the pile of books and blows out the candle. She picks up the black scarf printed with flowers and places it around her shoulders like a shawl. She walks to the lit candle that was placed at the left end of the line radiating from the sugar cane across the stage.

Her voice in voiceover says: I was born in Detroit, Michigan.
She blows out the candle and says. Je suis née à Detroit, Michigan.

She picks up her tape recorder, walks to the back candle that sits on the chalk line.
and blows it out. Her voice in voiceover says:

My mother was born in Selma, Alabama.
She says: Ma mère est née à Selma, Alabama.

With the two candles and the tape recorder, she walks to the front candle on the chalk line radiating from the sugar cane and blows that out.

Her voice in voiceover says: My father was born in Port-au-Prince, Haiti.
She says: Mon père est né à Port-au-Prince, Haïti.

She disappears to where the first candle went and blows that one out. She replaces the four candles unlit next to the silver bucket of sugar cane. She presses play on the tape recorder and reads it like a book.

It says: I was born in Detroit, MI. My mother was born in Selma, AL. My father was born in Port-au-Prince, Haiti. In 1996, I took a translation course at New York University . . .

She says, into the book of the tape recorder in her hands:
J'ai suivi un cours de traduction à l'université de New York.
Mon projet final était la traduction du texte <<*A vol d'ombre*>>
du poète Jacqueline Beaugé.
Overall, it is a poem of love.

On the back wall, a projection of the book title: A vol d'ombre by Jacqueline Beaugé translated by Gabrielle Civil. These words stay the same while the translation in English changes:

At the flight of the shadow
At the theft of the shadow
At shadow flight
As the shadow flies
As the shadow steals away.

As these words glow on the screen, the lights dim.
One final voice over plays of the black woman translator
singing her lullaby to the Haitian woman poet.
Bon soir mère, madame fais do . . .Fade out.
Only the half-moon of candles circling around the sugar cane
remain flickering.

(*Fin.*)

Vacant Night

by Ashraf Fayadh

Translated from Arabic by

Mona Kareem

Under the falling horror of my night
all suspicious questions reside
declaring that the night will go on . . . unanswered.
No difference . . . for all night is one
maneuvering desires of thunder
and joy of clouds, clothed in loneliness.

the star-shepherds find it strange
that I exploit time
throwing future intoxications
behind my steps.
The clubs went on watching my worries
trying to avoid the slaps which no longer miss
the way to my face . . .
That is my destiny,
my destiny is to intersect
with all these suspicious fantasies
between cloud, thunder,
and astronomical objects in exile . . .

I claim to have mastered
the act of raining on sand grains
in order to make a memorial for mankind.

I try to remember
where is the way to sand?
and where is man on the bodily margin of night?
There is a difference . . . to look for the body of night
and to search your body for a longing for night.

There's a difference
in longing to visit a woman of almond
and recite to her from a body
made nervous by the depth of night.
There's a difference
if you ever find the eyes
that could host your decaying body in their restfulness.

It is a shame to recite the body
and to go against a constitution
of sacred words
for you need the heart
to love
and the heart
will only be born when humans return

the rain had overloaded you with
expensive advertisement pages
so you would search for sand grains,
the retired mud
and the horror of night

when hit with an object
cutting through eyes
unfamiliar with the taste of sleep.

What a shame
to look for a heart
when the rain has chosen you to be one
wide enough for all human kinds . . .
On the billboards of night,
the vacant night is searching for a lover
for someone fluent in the language of rain
and other human skills.

He is looking for a female
to bless her joys with the water of love
baptized by clouds
in the presence of a body
clayed with the smell of almond
to the sounds of ice cubes floating in the glass . . .
He is questioning the meaning of a dawn
drowning between the N, the feminine T, and the drunk H of endings.*

This body needs showers of soul-water,
clouds to make rain with,
words of longing,
and degrees recognized in exile
to practice all the love rituals
that could overthrow the Night regime.

Night,
you are inexperienced with time

lacking raindrops
that could wash away the remains of your past
and free you of chastity
and of a heart that can love and play
asserting your abandonment
of a flappy religion, a fraud revelation,
and of a faith in gods
who had lost their pride.

* *These letters refer to the feminine suffixes in the Arabic.*

Lord No and A Lullaby

by Kim Hyesoon

Translated from Korean by
Don Mee Choi

Lord No
Day Thirty Six

That you live with Lord No
he who descends from the mountain
that you sleep with the one who created you
You eat at the same table with
the one who claims to feed and raise you
the one who strips bare the world he has made
You live with him who
slaps your mommy's back
crinkles your mommy's brain map and
secretly locks the door to the outside world and discards the key
You fall asleep with the one
who shouts, Earn your keep!

You keep shouting in your head
I was born alone!
I have nothing to do with you!
Your sibling couldn't eat anything in front of him

She could only weep, vomit, and think of the waves of music
She wrapped herself in them
ran around in bed like a hedgehog
huffing and puffing from aphasia

Lord No does not Lord No and none and not at Lord No thus
    Lord No does not

Not none never Lord No nevertheless

Lord No who is not Lord No is never Lord No thus Lord No is
    Lord No of Lord No

Not Lord No is not Lord No thus Lord No is Lord No who will
    none to Lord No

Not Lord No is not Lord No thus Lord No is Lord No who will
    never Lord No to

        Lord No

Lord No who is not Lord No Lord No to Lord No is not Lord
    No thus is not Lord No

Lord No whom Lord No never not is not Lord No thus never
    none not to Lord No

Lord No who is not Lord No is never Lord No thus Lord No is
    Lord No who will not

        to Lord No

Lord No who does not none is not Lord No thus Lord No is Lord
No of Lord No

hence is Lord No who will not Lord No

Lord No who has never Lord No and none Lord No is not Lord
No thus Lord No is

Lord No of Lord No

None to Lord No then no to Lord No and never thus not Lord
No by Lord No is not

not Lord No is not Lord No to Lord No

Do not and not. Lord No is Lord No of Lord No from Lord No.
Lord No who did not to

Lord No was none like Lord No

That you live with Lord No
that you must end the prayer in his son's name
that you must live with the one who made the law
yet with his crocodile-like eyes
he tells you beware of a snake-like friend
that you live forever with Lord No who slaps your face
that you live with the naked light
who asks you whenever you undress
Aren't you ashamed?

A Lullaby

Day Thirty Seven

The mother of the child coddled her dead child in her arms.

She sang a lullaby.

This is the contents of her lullaby.

Sleep, sleep my baby, die soon so you'll be at ease, so you won't have to cry.

The mother of the child dug and buried her child in the middle of her room.

She also buried her child in the ceiling. Buried in the wall. Buried in her pupils.

Nobody knew the name of the child's mother but they knew the child's name.

Horoscope and Poem Standing on Fallujah's Door

by Kishwar Naheed

Translated from Urdu by
Mahwash Shoaib

Horoscope

You have the empty vessel of trust
and I am thirsty for forty years.
You have the magnifying glass to see into the future
and I in the desert of today am searching for a highway.
You have the deep shade of calm
and I have been burnt in the sun of disquietude.
You have the oars of a love like dew
and I like the hand of a man drowning at sea
am apparent as the twilight of momentary life.
In your fist are shining the fireflies of dreams
and in my hands sleeping sadness
wants to descend in my body through the lines of my hand.
The spring of your lips is knocking
the closed door of my heart which
even the storm could not open
was not swept even in the flood
did not shake with even the quake.
Holding the empty vessel of trust
how long will you keep standing at this door!

Poem Standing on Fallujah's Door

What should I do with those poems
I had written against
running blood and tyranny
for blood is constantly running
and tyranny, it keeps increasing

What should I do with those poems
in which the sounds of the crying of
scared, wounded children echoed,
for now everywhere groans and sighs
lacerate my ears

What should I do with those poems
I had written on
flying birds and laughing girls,
for now girls even cheaper than plunder
are bought and sold

What should I do of those poems
that my ancestors wrote
they challenged god and were called genius
but if alive today, would be flayed as heretics

Tell me, what should I do of that truth
that cannot be told on earth
that cannot be read in the heavens
that cannot be printed in newspapers
and if said in front of people
they call you

uneducated and tactless

Tell me
what should I do of this heritage
wrapped in the corner of my dupatta
that is like an empty candle in my hands
for the blazing flame in it
followed those people
who were canny and sycophant
I see severed heads even in my dreams
Maybe it is time for my poems to desert

From Trinity to Trinity
(excerpt)
by Kyoko Hayashi

Translated from Japanese by
Eiko Otake

<Trinity Site> is on the outskirts of the town of Alamogordo, 190 kilometers southeast of Albuquerque.[1] Soon after the streetlights, smoky with morning mist, were put out, our car drove into a dusty wilderness. Our view opens up in all directions, and to the left of the road, mountain peaks far in the east start to shine a golden color. The rising sun is behind the mountains, and the slopes that have the sun on their backs lie in black shadow. On the right, as time passes, the faces of the mountains in the west show a light expanding from their peaks toward their grassy bottoms. As we drive, the ridgeline of the mountains begins to change, so that the sun goes down behind a mountain and then rises again above another mountain. Responding to that, the mountains in the west become dark and, at the next moment, grass on the surface of the same mountains shines like a girl's blond hair.

Soon grassy areas wet with dew waved like river fog, and the morning sun showed its complete face. Forty minutes have passed since we left the hotel. There are no cars coming toward us. On the earth or in the sky, I see no human or other living creature.

A little after 8:00 a.m., we arrived at a rest area on a highway that was constructed by putting together thick planks of lumber. This is the first building we have seen since we started our drive today. This rest house is built out of logs without any windows or doorways.

It is only equipped with water and a bathroom. The bathroom alone has walls and a door where an Indian man stands as a guard. Tsukiko asked me, I want to smoke, is it OK? And she then drove to a concrete parking lot in front of the building. There were several trucks and passenger cars. A man, his boot resting on a truck window frame, was taking a nap. It seems he had been driving a long distance. Tsukiko parked her car next to his truck.

Smoking a cigarette, Tsukiko crosses a wooden bridge toward the rest stop, which is built above ground. Looking back from an information board that had a sign with red letters, she said, here, they say Watch Out for Rattlesnakes. Surprised, I asked, you mean *rattlesnakes*?

Yes, it says rattlesnakes. "Do not step off the concrete paths and wooden bridges. It is forbidden to let pet dogs loose. If you do not follow these rules and get bitten by a snake, you are responsible for any damage." OK? Tsukiko reminded me again as the morning chill was making my back curl.

Following Tsukiko I walked over the bridge and stood facing the wilderness to the west. The field stretched up to the foot of the mountains. I took a deep breath. Under these grasses, snakes hide themselves waiting for their prey. The warning told us not to walk away from the bridge. So perhaps there are snakes right underneath me in the grass, which I might be able to see from cracks in the wooden bridge.

How might the snakes' bodies look and what color are their eyes? Blue? Red? Like Fat Man and Little Boy, rattlesnakes are killers, so they probably have no wasteful lines in their bodies. In the wilderness of the West, I imagined a rattlesnake from Steinbeck's <<The Snake.>>

Steinbeck describes a rattlesnake that is aiming at a catch: <See!

He keeps the striking curve ready. A rattlesnake is a cautious, almost cowardly animal.> <The mechanism of its body being extremely delicate> this Texas-born protagonist of <<The Snake>> is a <dusty grey,> big snake <nearly five feet long.>

It looks like an animal perfectly made for a wilderness that is just starting to dry in the morning sun. It would not be strange if a five-foot long snake were looking up at Tsukiko and me. I do not need a five-foot rattlesnake. So I walked only on the concrete path and the wooden bridge and then got into the car.

The sun started to hurt our eyes. It was two hours and forty minutes since we had departed, and the scenery was starting to show subtle changes. The field, looking like a scrubbing brush, is still the same, but now I see scattered plants as tall as boys. A man who is familiar with the area would know his location by looking at the plants, but the <Trinity Site> is a hidden place not listed on maps. The only things that made us guess we were near our destination were an iron tower on a plateau ahead of us and a huge, parabolic, dish-shaped antenna.

It looks like we're here, Tsukiko said and slowed down her car. Fifty meters ahead of us are several cars.[2] A female officer, who was talking with a driver, raised her hand to order us to stop. She comes by and with a knock on our car window says, the <Trinity Site> is under U.S. Army jurisdiction. Please open your window. Ahead on the road, which she says is under military jurisdiction, is a wilderness. A fence built with barbed wire and logs is open. This fence is the gate of the <Trinity Site.>

The officer saw Tsukiko and me and confirmed, two of you? Then she offered us two printed papers. Read and sign, she states. It is <13 Rules on Visiting.> The gate opens at 8:30 a.m. and last entry is at 2:00 p.m. If a person enters the gate at 2:00 p.m., visits <Ground Zero,> and walks around within the fence, he/she will not leave the gate before 3:00 p.m. The night falls fast in wilderness and that would make a visit after 2:00 p.m. dangerous. As if predicting and dealing with such danger, there was a clearance of responsibility, <from here on you are leaving the jurisdiction of New Mexico. If you have an accident, the State of New Mexico bears no responsibility.> This was on a bulletin board. Then came a printed <Rules on Visiting.> The fence is easy to jump over, but they gave us a round of warnings:

—Demonstrations, picketing, sitting, marches, political speeches, and other such activities are forbidden.

—No carrying of any arms on the White Sands Missile test site.

—Do not pick up any <Trinitite> in <Ground Zero>. Not only is the National Monument <Trinity> radioactive, but the plants are also.[3]

—Be careful of snakes. Rattlesnakes have been seen at <Ground Zero> and the McDonald Lunch House.

—Leave your pets in your car. When doing so, keep windows open. High heat can kill your pet quickly.

We signed the paper and were allowed to enter. We drove on a long narrow road that was bordered by a fence. Once again, an officer instructed our car to stop. From that point on vehicles were no longer allowed and the <Trinity Site> starts.

In the rules we read, <Trinitite> referred to all materials in the <Trinity Site> such as stones, glass pieces, grass, flowers, soil, and sands. The <Trinity Site> means a small wasteland surrounded by fences about three meters high that is itself within a wasteland. At the approximate center is <Ground Zero,> where the plutonium bomb was detonated for its explosion test. At <Ground Zero> is a <National Historic Monument.> It is a quadrangular pyramid constructed of stones. It is about three meters high.[4] In short, everything in the <Trinity Site,> even a little dirt on the back of our shoes, is a national secret put on display.

In the fenced area is an open space that could encompass six or seven baseball fields. I hear that areas around here, including those outside the fence, are missile test sites. I do not think *White Sands*, printed on the tourist photo guide, is the same place as *White Sands*, the missile test site, but I learn that "more than 42,000 missiles and rockets have been fired at the range since 1945." There was a warning, "Be careful: in the firing range explosives might be found in the ground. This is a known fact."

A small booklet, <<Trinity Site 1945–1995,>> says:

> Radiation levels in the fenced ground zero are low. On average the levels are only ten times greater than the region's natural background radiation. A one-hour visit to the inner fenced area will result in a whole body exposure of one-half to one milliroentgen. To put this in perspective, a U.S. adult receives an average exposure of 90 milliroentgens every year from natural and medical sources. For instance, the Department of Energy says we receive between 35 and 50 milliroentgens every year from the sun and from 20 to 35 milliroentgens every year from our food.—The decision is yours.[5]

The danger is well explained.

If a person stays in the fenced area for one hour, 0.5-1 milliroentgen will be added to his body. Since the average American adult takes in 90 milliroentgens per year, one cannot say that the radiation a person receives at the <Trinity Site> is low.

Getting out of the car holding a mineral water bottle, the only thing allowed, we walked into the fenced area. There are about two hundred visitors. Many are with families, and I spot fathers holding children's hands. Visitors walk looking down. Maybe they are careful of the needles of desert plants and small radio-active weeds at their feet. The only things that move in this wilderness are humans walking in the <Trinity Site.> In the treeless field, it seems even a bird cannot make a nest.

I tried to listen to the quiet of the wilderness. I wanted to hear the small but lively sound of popping seeds from the pods warmed by the sun. Even the sandy noise an insect makes as it falls into a pit of ant lions would do. I wanted to hear the kind of noise a living thing makes.

I walked to <Ground Zero.> When I reached the outer circle of visitors surrounding the stone memorial, I stopped. I turned my face to look around. As far as I could see was a field with no place to hide. The only things higher than the ground were humans, the fences surrounding the <Trinity Site,> red mountains on the horizon, and one thing more. In the center, in front of me, is a memorial to <Ground Zero.>

From this point in July, fifty years ago, the flash of light of the atomic bomb ran all directions in the desert. I heard, on the day of the experiment, it had been raining hard since morning, unusual in New Mexico. The experiment was carried out in the heavy rain.[6]

The flash of light boiled the downpour and, with that white froth, ruined the fields, burned the helpless mountains, and shot up to the sky. And then silence. Without time to defend and fight back, the wilderness was forced into silence.

From the bottom of the ground, from the exposed red faces of faraway mountains, from the brown waste-land, the waves of silence came lapping and made me shudder. How hot it must have been—.

Until now as I stand at the <Trinity Site,> I have thought it was we humans who were the first atomic bomb victims on Earth. I was wrong. Here are my senior *hibakusha*.[7] They are here but cannot cry or yell.

Tears filled my eyes.

I have always been aware of being a *hibakusha*. But as soon as I started walking through the small passage within the fenced area led by a guide, my always-present awareness of being a victim disappeared from my mind. It was as if I became a fourteen-year-old again. I may have been walking toward an unknown <Ground Zero> as though I were someone from <the time> before August 9, but it was when I stood in front of the memorial that I was truly exposed to the atomic bomb.

Looking back, I did not shed a tear on August 9. As I ran with the pack of people whose hands, feet, faces no longer looked human, no tears came to me. Like ants on a midsummer road, there was a line in the burned field of Urakami.[8] It was a line of people who could walk and had come for treatment. Facing that line was a doctor at work. The head of the doctor, who was sitting on a stone, was also covered by a bandage. Nagasaki was completely ruined. I could see all the way to the sea. The only things higher than the ground were people. I ran and ran, glancing at scenes lit by fire.

Three days later my mother came to look for me from the village where my family had moved to escape the war. On the way, she met the mobilized students going to rescue the victims. My mother told them the name of the place I worked and asked them to get my bones if they saw some small ones.

When she found me without a wound, my mother said, you are alive. She embraced me and cried. But I still did not shed my tears. For the first time, here at Trinity, however, I might be crying with the human tears that I did not shed on August 9. Standing on the land that speaks no words, I shivered, feeling its pain. Until today, I have lived with merciless pains that hurt both my mind and body. But it could have been the pain of the skin that grew from August 9. Here in this desert I had momentarily forgotten my life as a *hibakusha.* Over the land that keeps its silence I must have been seeing the scene of the day when I ran away. I have tried to suppress that scene in my mind over many years. Me on that fatal day.

I saw the back of an old man walking toward <Ground Zero.> Away from any other groups of people, he walks alone with a cane. Is he about seventy-two or seventy-three years old? He is tall and was built with a sturdy frame. He looks like a wounded veteran. Maybe because he has bad eyes, he wears darkly shaded glasses. Nobody accompanies him. Perhaps he wished to visit <Ground Zero> while he can still travel and join a bus tour. I was attracted to the sorrowful old man. How has he lived his life since the War? Since he came all the way expressly to visit the <Trinity Site>, like the old man in the museum and Tsukiko's husband, this man probably also fought in World War II.

The man walked, letting his stick investigate the <Trinity Site>, and at the outside of the crowd that circled the monument, he stopped. Resting both hands on the top of his stick, the man is looking at the monument from far away.

Three or four boys wearing camouflage clothes run by the old man. Another boy is playing alone, throwing a red Frisbee into the blue sky.

Fat Man, which was in the Atomic Museum in the Air Force Base until yesterday, was brought here during the night and is now on display inside the fence. This is the same style, a brother-like bomb, as the plutonium bomb used for the test explosion. It *returns* home twice a year.

Tsukiko and I were walking hand-in-hand. In the grass were a few five-petaled flowers similar to the Japanese *quince* that I see often in the Japanese hills and fields. Yellow and shiny flowers are also blooming.

Tsukiko and I sat and looked at the flowers that bloomed close to the ground. I wonder if Kana is alive, Tsukiko asked me suddenly. She is fine, I said.

After looking at the crater blasted by the test explosion, we walked to the exit. There was a crowd near the exit, which was also an entrance. We did not notice it when we came in, but there was a wooden table, on which there were broken parts of instruments used in the test explosion, an alarm clock and pieces of iron parts. A female officer was putting a Geiger counter on the alarm clock. The hand shook vigorously and the detector started ringing.

These were the instruments used in the test on that rainy day. Radiation still remains, she explains, pointing the Geiger counter at the clock's hand. Like a wave, the sound becomes bigger and smaller. Oh! The Americans shake their heads. They seem to be moved by the power that remains a half-century later. Is it not something? Tsukiko and I also nodded our heads.

The officer looked content with the reception. I was watching in awe with the people who gathered around the table. Realizing how ridiculous it is for me to be among them, I felt like I wanted to put that Geiger counter on my body as a demonstration. When it starts to ring Gaaaaaaaaaa they would be surprised, I thought.

How long radiation remains once it is released on Earth varies depending on the materials, but they say it lasts almost eternally. My acquaintance in France told me that upon entering the room of Madame Curie, the detector still starts to ring.

Next to the rusted instruments were small stones in a glass container. About one centimeter in diameter, the small stones are perfectly round. The stones as a whole look gray, but looking closer, they reveal grains of white, brown, green, and red sand. The officer pointed to one stone that had no shine, and started to explain:

"This small stone was made when the atomic bomb explosion blew up the earth's sand and soil, which danced together in the air, mingled, melted in the high heat, and got jammed together into a ball shape. We call this small stone a pearl," he said. The stone was a perfectly shaped sphere.

The crew of Bockscar that attacked Nagasaki wrote, <on the ground many more things were happening than what was seen at the test explosion in the desert of Alamogordo, New Mexico.> Did the people who were melted in the high heat also become small stones and dance in the air? Someone told me the bones of young people shine pink. I wished the bones of my dead friends would at least become lovely pink pearls.

In front of the table displaying <pearls,> local journalists were preparing for an interview. Two Japanese men were standing surrounded by people. They are *hibakusha* from Hiroshima who will be interviewed. Among the American onlookers, the two men in T-shirts stood with tense expressions.

With their heads up, they stood straight.

1. Approximately 120 miles.
2. Approximately 165 feet.
3. Trinitite is the name given to the soil that was fused into glass-like objects by the heat from the Trinity atomic bomb test. Trinitite is typically a grayish or light olive green color, with a smooth, fused top surface on one side and the irregular texture of the sandy desert surface on the other side. While the Bureau of Atomic Tourism website (www.atomictourist.com) warns that Trinitite is "still radioactive and must not be picked up," it is reported that by the early 1950s the government had excavated and buried almost all of the Trinitite remaining at the site. On one commercial website, Mineralogical Research Co. (www.minresco.com), Trinitite pieces are called collectors' items and are sold as "Products of the First Atomic

Bomb Explosion." This site claims that Trinitite was "highly radioactive in 1945," but that its radioactivity at the present is "virtually zero."

4. Three meters is nearly ten feet.
5. The same information is found at the website, White Sands Missile Range Public Affairs Office, "Trinity Site Pamphlet."
6. It turns out that Hayashi's description here is not completely historically accurate, the details and significance of which I discuss in the Afterword of the book *From Trinity to Trinity.*
7. Hibakusha is the Japanese word for a victim (or victims) of the atomic bombings.
8. Urakami was the epicenter of the atomic bomb explosion on August 9, 1945. It was the site of Urakami Cathedral.

Epistles to the Dead

Dagmawi Woubshet

In an untitled painting created in the late 1990s, Trevor Makhoba, the late South African painter, captures the havoc wrought by AIDS in his country and in many other parts of the global south. The canvas depicts a burial procession, which is not an unconventional subject for a painting. What's disturbing about Makhoba's burial scene, however, is that the people carrying the casket and watching the procession are all toddlers. Innumerable, the children file out to the horizon carrying caskets grossly disproportional to their bodies, the white diapers they wear in sharp relief against the muted tones of the painting. With gripping simplicity, Makhoba conjures up the plight of the masses of children who were losing their parents to AIDS at the time, the grief they had to bear. The idea of young children as pallbearers is both haunting and confounding. Since children cannot physically carry coffins, Makhoba's painting compels the viewer to ask, then, how do they bear their loss? How do children mourn without recourse to the funerary rites and rituals that shore us up as adults? What is their vocabulary of death, their grammar and calendar of loss? And, how do these particular children stigmatized by AIDS—orphaned not just by their parents, but by the world around them—carry out the work of mourning?

To begin to answer these questions, I have found great insight in the work of Sudden Flowers.[1] Founded in 1999, Sudden Flowers was the first AIDS art collective in Ethiopia, and began as a collaboration among the American photographer Eric Gottesman and Salamawit Alemu, Yamrot Alemu, Biniyam Mesfin, Hana Mesfin, Amsale Shiferaw, and Asrat Tessema, Ethiopian children between the ages of nine and seventeen orphaned by AIDS. Using a variety of media—letters, photographs, films, public installations, performances—this pioneering collective has produced remarkable narratives of AIDS over fifteen years, which provide an interior perspective into how children have borne this calamity. It is a body of work that transcends the myopic and overdetermined discourse—governmental, NGO, public health, news media—that has narrowly framed the experience of AIDS orphans, often obscuring the agency, resilience, and depth of perception with which children have confronted this catastrophe.

Between 1999 and 2004, the children of Sudden Flowers wrote over fifty letters addressed to their deceased parents. In their extraordinary intimacy, these epistles to the dead became a powerful form of mourning and self-expression for these children, as well as an integral part of the group's creative repertoire. I call these texts "epistles" because they are letters addressed to someone in particular and because of their literariness; many of them read like verse. My English translations do not fully capture the poetry and lyric intimacy of the original letters in Amharic, partly because I have opted for translations that closely follow the original grammar and wording of the letters in order to maintain the integrity of the children's own utterances of loss. Nor can the translations convey the experience of reading the original letters in the children's own handwriting and language. Since many of these epistles are by budding writers whose penmanship and literacy have yet to settle—because of their young age and intermittent schooling—there are many mischaracterizations of the Ethiopic alphabet and vocabulary: there are words missing characters, words that are not legible, and sentences and paragraphs without punctuation marks. On the first pass, these flaws might bring the reader to a halt. I had to reread many of the letters word by word, modifying characters and tweaking diacritics in order to capture the intended sound and meaning of a word; and line by line, disarticulating strings of sentences. Despite these constraints in translation, I hope the English renditions still impart the children's expressions of loss, longing, and life.

Salamawit Alemu was nine years old when she drafted her epistles, three letters that embody her personal loss and anguish as well as exemplify common themes and terms of loss expressed in many of the children's letters. Salamawit stood out as a member of Sudden Flowers, not merely because at nine she was the youngest founding member of the collective, nor because of the incalculable hardships and trauma she endured as a child. In her keenly reflexive and performative work a strong sense of her own agency comes through. For example, she renamed herself at age seven, changing her first name from Rut to Salamawit, meaning She Is Peace. And she assumed another persona, Beti, in Gottesman's portfolio of portraits of her, as well as in her own self-portraits. When writing to her dead parents, she crafted letters as both Rut, the name given to her at birth, and Salamawit, the name she gave herself, each version imbued with grief and empowered self-expression. The epistle that she authored as Salamawit reads:

> To My Dear Mother
>
> My dear beloved mother how are you? Except for the thought of you and longing for you I am fine. Because now you are not living by my side with such intense feeling my stomach gets very very disturbed. Now when a mother hugs her boy or her girl I wish my mother was here I could also be hugged like this I say. Because you are not here by my side now no one cheers

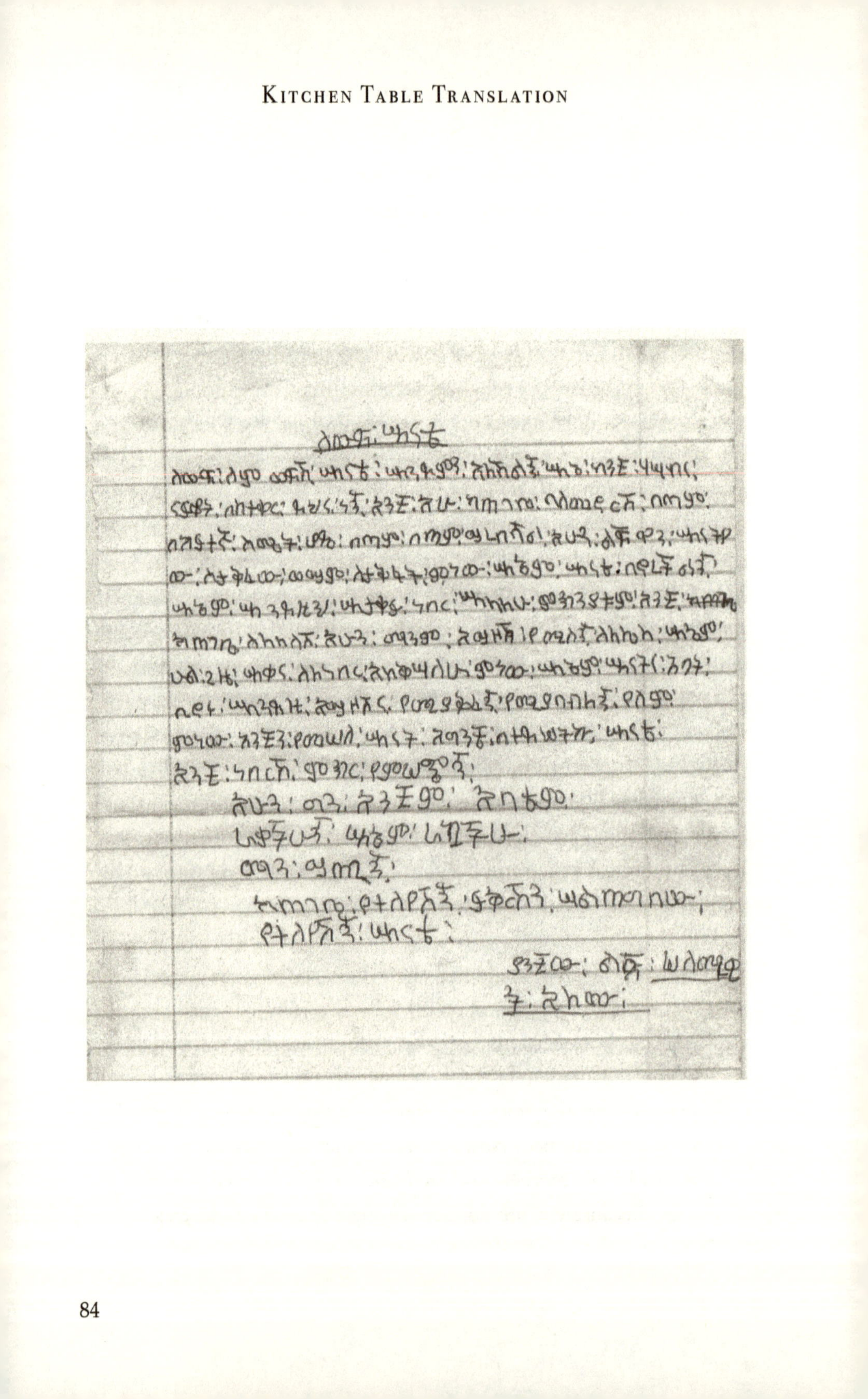

> me up and because I always get jealous I cry. If my mother and father were here, like this, there is no one to cheer me up, to hug me, to console me. I wish I could find a mother like you and be happy. Mommy, you were the one who gave me advice. But now both you and my father are far from me and I am far from you. Who comes close to me?
>
> Separated from my side before I was full of your love separated from me my mother.
>
> Your child,
> Salamawit Alemu

Salamawit's letter exhibits the pathos and vexed grammar typical of these epistles to the dead: a form in which bereaved children hold an intimate conversation with their deceased parents and mediate the interface between life and death. Salamawit's epistle, like several others, begins with a generic salutation—"My dear beloved mother how are you?"—and, more specifically, with the generic salutation of Amharic letters addressed to a beloved the writer has not seen for some time: "Except for the thought of you and longing for you I am fine." These are two basic conventions of letter writing in Amharic with which these children would have been familiar. But there is something disconcerting about these salutations in the children's letters. Although standard in addressing the living, in these letters they hail the dead. Delineated from the start is the tension between the present orientation of the letter as a form of communication among the living, and the irrevocable absence of the recipients of these letters, who are dead addressees incapable of replying. Even as they rehearse the basic greetings of the Amharic letter, these epistles conjure an absent addressee who has departed, troubling the fixed distinction between the living and the dead.

Throughout the collection of letters, the children repeatedly characterize the relationship between themselves and their dead parents as a separation that is not ultimate. Although in reality the separation may be final and irrevocable, in the letters that separation is still tentative, in flux, unfixed. The reiterated term and trope for death is "separation," while the term "death" appears, astonishingly, in only one letter. Amharic has a repertoire of phrases that use separation as a euphemism for death—*kezee alem bemot teleye* (from this world by death he's separated), *kezee alem teleye* (from this world he's separated), and, pruned down further, *kealem teleye* (from the world he's separated)—but the separation is qualified to signify, categorically, another world the dead inhabit. When the word "separation" shows up in these letters, however, it is never in the context of these common adult expressions that mark the divide between the world of the living and the world of the dead. Furthermore, none of the letters use the most popular Amharic euphemism for death: *maref*, "to rest." Thus, when Salamawit closes her letter with the lyrical words "Separated from my side before I was full of your love separated from me my mother," we have to consider closely what "separated" denotes in this loaded line and not presume that the term signifies in the same way it does for adult speakers of the language.

It is worth noting how these epistles account for the separation between the living and the dead. The children measure the space that divides them and their parents in terms that are contiguous—"not living by my side," "not here," "far from me," as Salamawit writes—but give no indication as to where their parents have gone. Given the deeply religious character of Ethiopians, and the almost automatic use of religious condolences in speaking about death, one expects to see the children resort to that vocabulary and imagery to characterize their parents' posthumous abode, but they don't. Their letters employ a trope of separation that is relative rather than absolute, eschewing the language of scripture and religious condolences that are conclusive about where the dead dwell. Consider, for instance, how Salamawit, in another letter to her mother (this one signed as Rut) inscribes death as a tentative separation. Addressing her mother, she writes: "But you having left begging you are now in a better place. Mommy now will you not come to see us?" Rut imagines her mother to have gone to "a better place" where she is no longer a beggar enduring that life of extreme hardship. Nevertheless, "a better place"—a common Christian phrase to signify heaven—is not used here in a religious sense; in fact, the question that immediately follows defies Christian eschatology, since it conceives of the dead as inhabiting a contiguous space and time, as capable of being summoned back and physically reuniting with the bereaved.

Some of the most arresting portions of these letters are precisely the moments when the children demand that their deceased parents materialize themselves either in person or as embodied tokens of parental care and affection. In her letter, Amsale says to her mother: "What I want to tell you after this is about my school. I have good grades. Now in the first semester I came in second. And in the second semester, well, I think I will come in between first and third. Make sure you send me the prize, okay, Mommy?" Bereket Muluneh asks of his mother, "Today you know is a holiday. Give me money." Heywot Umer, in one of her two letters, makes an insistent plea for her mother's material care and embodied presence: "Now the reason I am writing this letter to you is because my clothes are wearing out and I want you to buy me clothes. And shoes and everything, just come and I will tell you, don't you think? If you came and we talked or played how thrilled I would be. Therefore before spending a day or night hurry and come. I love you very much. I will wait for you, ok?" The conflation of the living and the dead may stem partly from the conflation of the grammar of letter writing, which is the present tense, and the grammar of loss, which is geared toward the past tense or the subjunctive. But that conflation also reflects these children's particular, unfixed sense of the interface between the living and the dead, which is why they make these kinds of temporal and material demands on their parents.

Along with a provisional sense of separation, the letters share other notable features. One is their characterization of loss in somatic terms as the loss of intimacy with the parent's body. Salamawit says, "Now when a mother hugs her boy or her girl I wish my mother was here I could also be hugged like this I say. Because you are not here by my side now no one cheers me up and because I always get jealous I cry." This is a striking scene, to which she returns in each of her three letters. Writing to her father, she says, "now because you are not near me when everyone hugs his child I begin to covet and because you are not near me I am very mournful." And as Rut, she writes to her mother: "And now when a father hugs his child, when a mother is going to the market with her child, at that time, I remember you." Seeing other parents physically intimate with their children triggers a range of intense feelings in this author: longing, jealousy, crying, coveting, and mourning, all prompted by the absent parental touch the child craves. There is another telling context in which the word "hug" shows up, this time as a metaphor to characterize the new caretaker in the children's lives. Amsale writes: "My name is Amsale Shiferaw. I am a student in the 8th grade. I don't have a father and a mother. I live hugged by an organization." These children yearn for the physical care and affection expressed by a parent's hug, so much so that they extrapolate from that embodied act to other forms of caregiving, like that provided by the organization that now sponsors them.

Another striking characteristic of the loss in these epistles features time, perhaps best expressed in Salamawit's closing line—"Separated from my side before I was full of your love separated from me my mother"—with its eloquent articulation of the calendar of bereaved children. The temporality of loss that Salamawit expresses is intimately linked to a foreshortened horizon of time that comes with youth. I read the phrase "before I was full of your love" to signify the author's reflexive sense of her own age, that her youth has somehow delimited the amount of her mother's love she could absorb. In another letter, Rut reiterates this same sentiment of lost futurity, delineating further the different temporal effects of loss on the child versus on the parent: "Before I could finish your love you left. You were finished with my love." The regret and resentment expressed in these lines suggest that the child feels betrayed by her age. As her intricate timeline of love and loss indicates, she feels that when her mother died she had not yet reached a certain threshold of time necessary to consummate a child's love for her mother, whereas her mother had been afforded that time. Others echo Salamawit's lament of lost time: "leaving her without finishing her love," writes Hana, describing herself in a missive to her mother, again characterizing loss partly as the loss of the future time necessary to forge a deeper bond with the parent. Other letters point to different temporal aberrations brought about by the loss of parents. Asrat had to leave school when her mother died and was held back when she eventually returned. She connects her grade retention and her mother's absence in the same line: "Isn't it sad, Mommy, if you were here, my education level and my age would have matched." Specifically, what Asrat is mourning in these lines—what's "sad"—is that her mother's absence has interrupted the normal progression of her development, misaligning the symmetry of age and grade level, a temporal tool by which children often evaluate themselves. Hence, there is a particular loss of time—a lost future to consummate love or a lost past to be in school—that is mourned in these letters in addition to the death of a parent.

The epistles take inventory of a range of losses experienced by these young children: as they lament the loss of their parent's physical body, as well as the care, affection, affirmation, and advice the parent provided, they also bemoan the loss of the old routines that structured the child-parent relationship. In Bereket Muluneh's letter, he strikes up an intimate, lyrical conversation with his mother, recalling the kinds of exchanges that once mediated their lives:

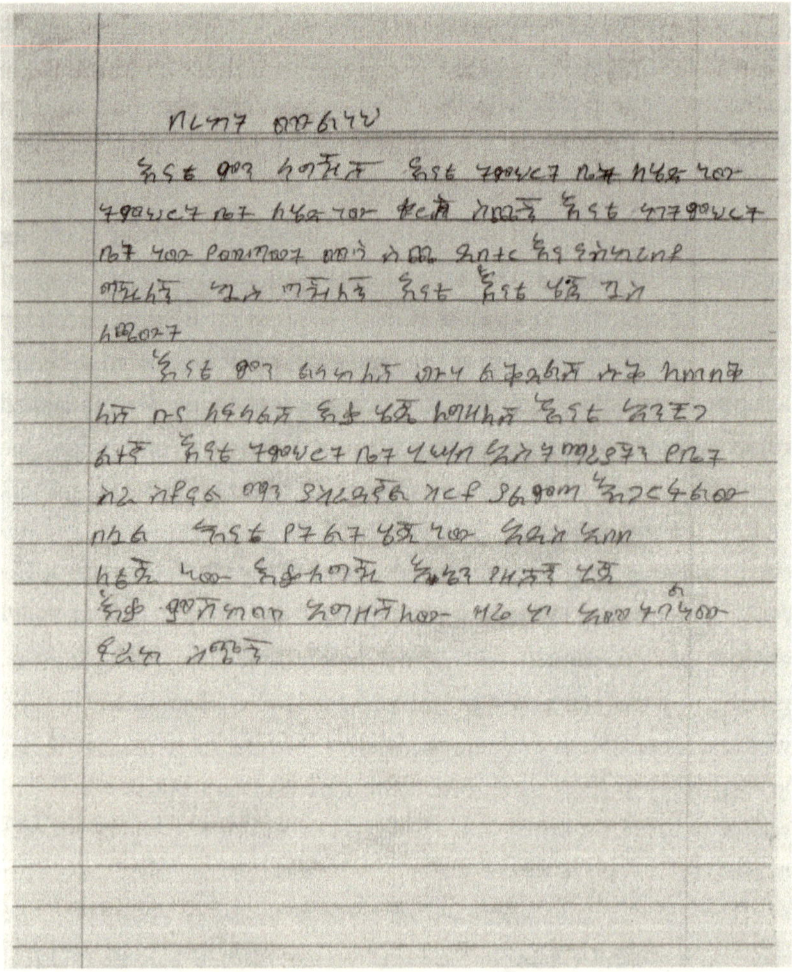

> [From] Bereket Muluneh
>
> Mother, how can I help you? Mother, I am about to go to school. I am about to go to school give me breakfast Mother. I just got back from school, give me lunch. Buy me a book and a pen. Buy me a ball. Mother, can I go and play ball? Mother, can I run an errand for you? Can I draw water for you? Watch the store for you? Brew coffee for you? Go and buy something for you? Mother, can we sleep together? Mother, at school our math teacher has given us an assignment, who's going to help me? I'll spank whoever comes to class without doing his homework, he said. Mother, where are you going? Are you going to Addis Ababa? To buy things? Take me with you. I will help you carry things. Today you know is a holiday. Give me money.

While most of these epistles open with the formal greetings of letter writing—which at the very least index a physical distance or separation between author and addressee—some like Bereket's eschew those conventions, breaking down further the barrier between the living and the dead. Here, the mother isn't merely the absent addressee of the missive, but a present interlocutor, however silent, partaking in the intimate colloquy of the lyric. The string of questions and the repeated apostrophe to his mother give Bereket's epistle an evocative aural rhythm, at the same time evoking the daily patterns of life. The action-oriented letter reprises not only the mother's authority and the essentials she provided her child (food, school supplies, toys, pocket money, physical comfort, protection) but also the roles and duties the child fulfilled for his mother (doing errands, performing household chores, helping her carry things). While the child's actions may seem routine and perfunctory, they are imbued with formative feelings. The desire to please and help one's parent by taking on certain duties, the delight to be had in running to the kiosk to fetch an item, the sensual experience of a coffee ceremony—say, the aroma of frankincense and roasting coffee beans—are among the everyday experiences, sensations, and pleasures the child is losing out on now, bereft of his mother.

Along with relaying the children's articulations of loss, the letters also convey the outcast status of these bereaved authors, who were of very poor background and moreover disparaged as AIDS orphans. The missives that I have referenced so far only gesture at the social status of these children. Salamawit asks, for instance, now that both her parents are gone, "Who comes close to me?"—which could also be translated as "Who dares comes close to me?" or "No one dares come close to me!" uttered in a tone that encapsulates the pariah status of people with AIDS at the time, including children. Even before they were orphaned, these children were no strangers to hardship. They lived at the very margins of Ethiopian society, often in the care of destitute mothers eking out an existence. And indeed other letters speak of the authors' social standing both before and after their parents' deaths, including new hardships borne by these children during the precarious intervening time between the deaths of their parents and their current foster care, left behind to live in abusive homes or forced to live in the streets.

Perhaps it's because these children were deprived of funeral rites that the feelings and prerogatives of mourning become insistent particularly in their epistles to the dead, why these set of letters are fixed on the body, why they insist on materializing the dead. Since they couldn't observe their parents' burials, these children use the resources of narrative to reckon with death, concretizing the dead on a piece of paper, giving their loss and longing material shape. Burial, Robert Pogue Harrison reminds us, "does not mean only the laying of bodies to rest in the ground. . . . in a broader sense it means to store, preserve, and put the past on hold."[2] He adds, "humans bury not simply to achieve closure and effect a separation from the dead but also and above all to humanize the ground on which they build their worlds and found their histories." Perhaps we can think of these epistles as undertaking the imperatives of burial, not only in humanizing the living world and holding onto the past, but also in establishing the bases for the children to found their histories. Like the pallbearers in Makhoba's painting, who despite their age insist on inhuming the dead, the children of Sudden Flowers commit themselves to archiving their dead, entering them into narratives that otherwise would not exist. By mourning the dead, by way of this humanizing act, the children of Sudden Flowers authorize themselves, using narrative to reclaim their inheritance and to survive.

ADDITIONAL LETTERS

8/8/92

For My Dear Mother,

Mother, I can never find someone like you. Because I know how burning with hardship you raised me. Ever since the day you left my father, without leaving me, without boredom, as long as your ability and age allowed it, you raised me. And, without being full of you, without you seeing me like this grown up, that you were separated from me makes me very sad. Mommy, let me remind you how you raised me back then. Carrying me on your back, when the rain pounded on you, selling boiled potatoes to raise me until I believe I was one or two years old. And you didn't rest when I got a little older. You'd take any day job you can find, that's how we began to live. After a long time, my father came again and saw us. But, Mommy, what kind of person is he? Why is it that people don't pity each other, love each other? My father is one of these people. Do you remember, per month 30 birr, he'd give us and leave. But you never waited for his handout. When we found food, we ate, when we didn't, we ate roasted chickpeas and drank water, and slept nestled together as if we were a single person. Isn't it sad, Mommy, if you were here, my education level and my age would have matched.

Yours, your loving, Asrat

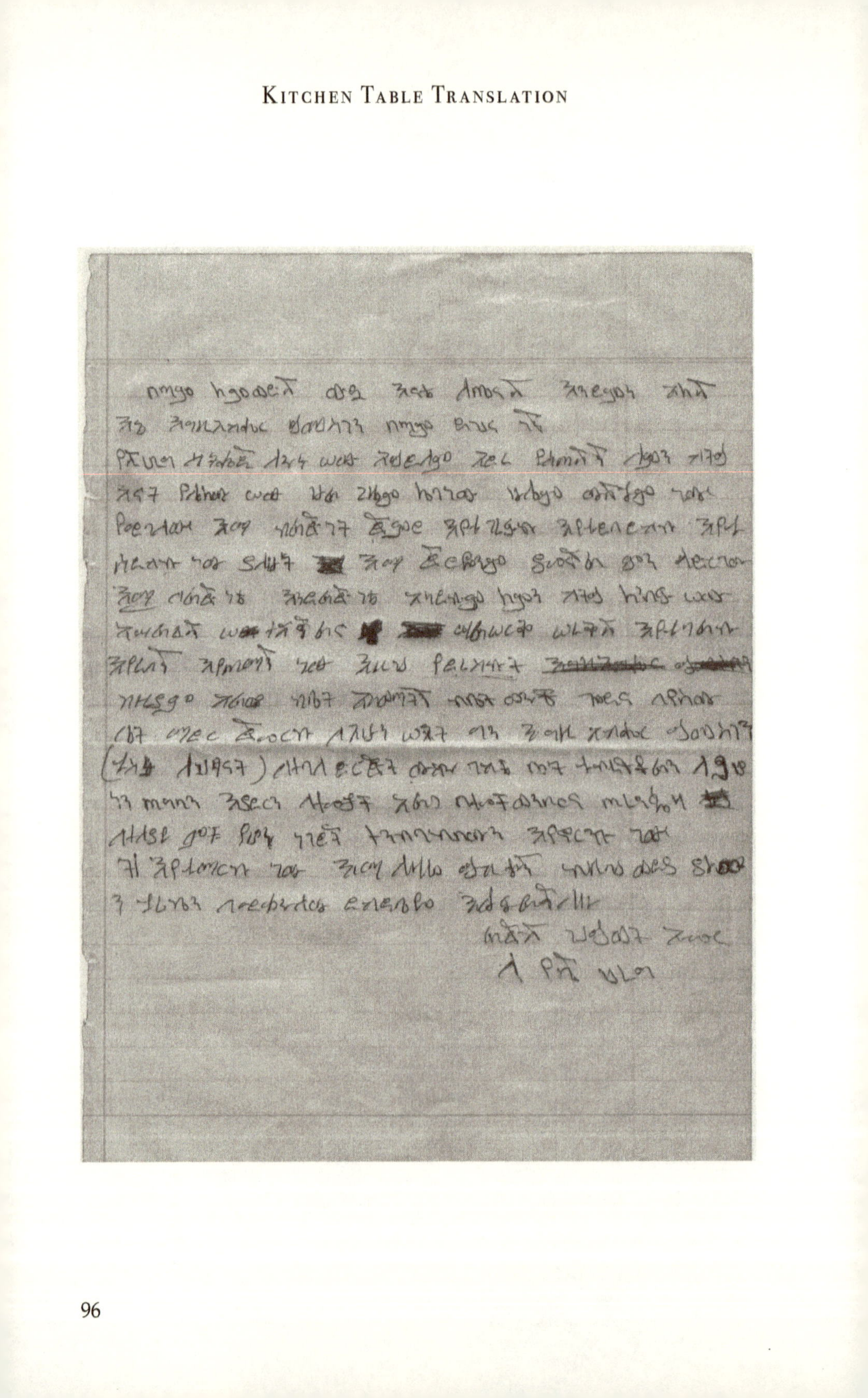

To my very beloved mother, how is your health, how are you? Me, praise to God, I am doing very well. Yeshi'hareg, when you left you did not leave me in the hands of a good person. If you ask why, a motherless child is always a thief, always a liar, that's what people say. Mom, from the beginning of my childhood until now, I have been spanked, beaten, cursed at. Mom, my ear also hurts. What shall I do to it? Mom, during my childhood, I did not live like a child. If you ask why, you have passed me on and given me up to a mean person. I am told that I steal, when I don't steal, I go hungry, I go thirsty, that's how I've come here. More than that, she made me leave her house. After leaving the house, I began to live on the streets, in people's houses. But at this time, praise God, I am in an organization called Tesfa Le'he'tsanat [Hope for Children], and living now in a house rented for us, nine of us, we go to bed on a full stomach, on a comfortable bed, comfortable seat, table, and several other comfortable things, they are caring for us. I am going to school. Mom, for today, let me stop here. In my next letter, I will send you what follows in my history.

Your child, Heywot Umer For Yeshi'hareg

First of all, thank you for giving me this opportunity. My name is Amsale Shiferaw. I am a student in the 8th grade. I don't have a father and a mother. I live hugged by an organization. The organization aids you until you are 18. After 18, they let you go. Us, me, we don't have anyone else assisting us. If they let me go, I don't know where I'll go. But now the organization is helping me. The organization has hired a nanny to supervise us. We appreciate anyone who would respond back to our letter. Amsale, ciao ciao

1. For an in-depth look at the work of Sudden Flowers, including the letters I cite in this essay, see, Eric Gottesman, *Sudden Flowers* (London: Fishbar, 2014).
2. Robert Pogue Harrison, *The Dominion of the Dead* (Chicago: University of Chicago Press, 2003), xi.

Translation: A Movement

Eléna Rivera

It's complicated keeping track of words.

Complicated keeping track of places, cultures, languages, traces.

Succession is a movement toward. Translation is a movement around.

When you're multi-lingual you have more words to choose from impossible to keep track of all the accretions.

In addition there's the language of the media, which is not your language but that you keep track of nonetheless (hence internalize).

When you're in-between languages you are in the chasm.

"You cannot solder an Abyss / With Air."

What happens if you try to get one language to pantomime another?

There's the responsibility to the text, and the responsibility to the author, and also the responsibility to the sign.

If words stop holding together, the abyss grows; that is grammar.

"Insert the Thing that caused it—"

Leaves are lucky they get to change colors, and we don't fault them for it either.

The pull of sound.

There's the person who learned one language then another and another, and the person who only learned one. There's the migrant and the rooted. There's the woman and the man. There's culling and there's extraction. Translation traverses and appreciates the differences.

I learned one language from ancient playwrights the other to survive the school-yard.

The school-yards kept changing, so there was no consistency.

Trying to fit in, to be like everybody else. The migrant wants to fit in with the rooted.

A displaced person is ___________.

At home languages were used interchangeably depending on the word available.

Understanding built through accretion, expression.

When I translate I can reinvent myself according to who I'm translating, like being an actor and playing a part.

"This babble shall not henceforth trouble me."

Playing a part can be useful when you don't know the language, otherwise the only thing left to you is the gesture.

One wants to be like everyone else in the schoolyard.

The words of another can shake us, being other, being not what we would say.

Translating we enter imaginatively into the world of another.

One has to make a huge effort.

Complicated enough to get the biography straight, to believe what you say about yourself, and what people say about you, but now you want to add the responsibility of speaking for another person into the mix?

I'd like to note here, I was never fond of mixed drinks. And was already "mixed," so you see now where my trouble lies.

What about the lies?

"You were born where?" "You grew up where?" Your parents are from where?"

The narratives of the body begin and, as I once wrote in a poem, the problematics of the verb "to be."

Mother says, we weren't immigrants we were refugees. What does the next generation say?

Words develop thick skins.

"Here is a coil with protestation!"

It is useful to coil words well, to soften the calluses in our eyes.

Give me your gesture so that I can understand your speech.

Change direction if a thought doesn't serve anymore. Discrimination becomes very important.

It is useful to listen to signals before making our selection.

What is on the outside is not the most interesting thing about us. The outside helps us to reconsider what is on the inside.

It is useful to begin the task of translation.

Consider other humans, their lives, their fears, joys, ambition, what food they eat, what artwork they encounter; it is useful to realize that one doesn't know anything.

Observe how one has learned to survive, it gives a clue to how we see the world.

It is useful to sit and stare out the window.

Sometimes words are completely foreign—it is useful to learn to listen.

I read the word "courage" and the outrage of that word keeps me going.

Note: Quotations are from Emily Dickinson and William Shakespeare.

Flicker and Flux

Versions of Heraclitus

Magda Kapa and Teju Cole

The pre-Socratic philosopher Heraclitus sounds strikingly modern. He wrote in fragments, of which only fragments survive, and this is part of the secret of his seemingly miraculous talent for compression. Not a word is wasted. Each aphorism strikes the ear like a mathematical formula: direct but gnomic, amoral and shorn of sentiment. One of the fragments might be read as an apologia for this mode of working: ὁ ἄναξ, οὗ τὸ μαντεῖόν ἐστι τὸ ἐν Δελφοῖς, οὔτε λέγει οὔτε κρύπτει ἀλλὰ σημαίνει. ("The lord whose oracle is at Delphi is neither clear nor cryptic. He signals.")

We were interested in doing "versions" or "readings" of Heraclitus rather than "translations" because we wished to test the fragments against modern expression. We tried to find a voicing balanced somewhere between poetry, vernacular speech, and laconic statement, always with an eye to brevity. We began with the ancient Greek text, and were guided by German, English, and modern Greek translations. What we aimed for was not a word-for-word rendering of each fragment, but a statement that retained the pith of the original while plundering it for new signals. Our version of fragment 49a, probably the best known of the Heraclitean fragments, illustrates our approach.

(The Greek fragments are taken from, and numbered as in *Die*

Fragmente der Vorsokratiker [9 ed. Berlin 1960], edited and translated by Hermann Diels and Walter Kranz.)

1

ἦθος ἀνθρώπῳ δαίμων. (119)
Human being, human daimon.

2

ξυνόν ἐστι πᾶσι τὸ φρονέειν. (113)
Mind is all, and in all.

3

ἐδιζησάμην ἐμεωυτόν. (101)
I have searched myself.

4

ὅσων ὄψις ἀκοὴ μάθησις, ταῦτα ἐγὼ προτιμέω. (55)
The things I can see or hear or study are the things I prefer.

5

ὀφθαλμοὶ γὰρ τῶν ὤτων ἀκριβέστεροι μάρτυρες. (101a)
Eyes see better than ears.

6

χρυσὸν γὰρ οἱ διζήμενοι γῆν πολλὴν ὀρύσσουσι καὶ εὑρίσκουσιν ὀλίγον. (22)
Goldminers mine earth mostly.

7

. . . μεταβάλλον ἀναπαύεται. (84a)
Things are at ease in flicker and flux.

8

τοὺς καθεύδοντας ἐργάτας εἶναι καὶ συνεργοὺς τῶν ἐν τῷ κόσμῳ γινομένων. (75)

Even sleepers are at work on the work of the cosmos.

9

ποταμοῖς τοῖς αὐτοῖς ἐμβαίνομέν τε καὶ οὐκ ἐμβαίνομεν, εἶμέν τε καὶ οὐκ εἶμεν. (49a)

We cannot enter a river at all. We are and are not.

Vão / Vòng
A Conversation with Katrina Dodson

Madhu H. Kaza

If someone had to inadvertently access my email inbox, I'm glad it was Katrina Dodson. During the week that I met Katrina in July 2016, I was teaching Elizabeth Bishop and writing about Clarice Lispector. Katrina, an Elizabeth Bishop scholar, is an acclaimed translator of Lispector. Last July we were both on a college campus in upstate New York for different reasons. One day I forgot to log out of my Gmail account on a public computer in a lab, and when Katrina came across the emails in my inbox with subject lines such as "crônicas draft" and "Self-Portrait in Green" (Marie NDiaye's novel, which she knew and loved), she momentarily confused the account for her own. When she told me about it later, it seemed as though that accident was itself a serendipitous introduction between us. I was delighted by our shared affinities, and my admiration for her work included a particular warmth that I feel for brilliant women writers and thinkers.

Katrina is well known for her tremendous, prize-winning translation of *The Complete Stories of Clarice Lispector.* I have a million questions for her about that project; she is the kind of person I'd want to sit and talk with for hours. Because time was limited when we conducted this interview via email and Google doc, because she has spoken more fully about Lispector in other contexts, and because of the focus of *Kitchen*

Table Translation, our exchange emphasized the intersections between translation, personal history, and cultural difference.

MHK: Can you talk about the relationship between your sense of identity and your work as a writer and translator from Brazilian Portuguese?

KD: I've always felt at odds with mainstream American culture and I think that has a lot to do with growing up in San Francisco and spending my formative years in majority non-white environments, both at home and at school, where a lot of my classmates had immigrant parents. My mother is from a rural village in north Vietnam and didn't come to the U.S. until 1975—she met my father in Saigon, where he was stationed as a Foreign Service officer in the late 1960s. She was able to bring part of her family over here after the war, so as a child I was surrounded by relatives speaking Vietnamese even though we spoke mostly English at home. I identify as Asian American, and "hapa" more specifically, the term that came from Hawaii and that's been adapted in California to identify people of part-Asian descent. I recently learned that in São Paulo, the word "*mestiço*" most commonly refers to mixed-race Asians, though people there usually assume I'm half Japanese, since Brazil has the largest population of Nisei Japanese.

This background has led me to seek out cultures and languages beyond the dominance of American English—maybe there's something appealing to me about being an outsider by choice rather than by default. I've always wanted to write more about Vietnam and from a more overtly mixed-race perspective, but as a result of some fateful decisions and general momentum, I ended up going much further in my relationship to Brazil.

My Asian heritage gets obscured by my European name, Katrina Dodson, especially since my writing and translations have mainly been focused on Brazil. People often respond with curiosity when they meet me in person and can tell that I'm part Asian, or at the very least, not white. They're usually pretty good at hiding their initial surprise, but then the question of my background eventually finds its way into the conversation. Sometimes people just assume that I'm Brazilian, and so it adds another level of surprise when I say I have no family connection to Brazil and that actually I'm half Vietnamese. I've thought about using my middle name, Kim, which my parents chose because it's both a Vietnamese and an American name (in Vietnamese, it means "metal" and can become "gold," "silver," or other metals depending on what compound word it forms). But then people assume that I'm half Korean, so it just makes things more confusing. I've sometimes wondered if I should add my mother's maiden name, to be Katrina Nguyen Dodson, to add that visibility to my name, and because I'm proud of my Vietnamese heritage. I wonder what effect that would have on how people view my work.

MHK: In your description of how you are read, there's a sense that your name is curiously illegible to people when they first encounter you and requires some further translation.

I'm curious about how you began translating from Brazilian Portuguese? Have you ever translated or thought about translating from Vietnamese? Do you have projects that connect you to your Asian background?

KD: I came to Portuguese rather by accident—by deciding to move to Brazil with a boyfriend back in 2003. I'd studied Vietnamese in college and spent a semester at Vietnam National University in Hanoi, but it's such a difficult language and was more daunting to try to master. When I first began my doctorate in Comparative Literature, I thought I'd be able to specialize in Brazilian literature in a comparative context, while also still being able to do some work with Vietnam. But the nature of academic scholarship meant I had to choose, and I chose Brazil, which has taken me down this path to translating Brazilian literature. It causes me some anguish to have such a close relationship to Brazilian culture, to often be mistaken for a Brazilian, and to feel less comfortable in Vietnamese contexts. I think in some ways, it's easier for me to be integrated into Brazilian culture, in part because Brazil is diverse like the U.S., and mixed-race people are the majority there. Plus, I don't take it personally when I make language mistakes or am pointed out as a gringa in Brazil. Vietnamese culture is much more exclusive, and mixed-race people are often not accepted as true Vietnamese. So it's more fraught for me when I try to make inroads into the language and culture—I'm much more sensitive to "failing" when I speak Vietnamese or when I don't know something. But I'm not done with Vietnam yet. I'd still like to go back and spend more time there and be able to really speak it with confidence. I'd like to write about my mother's life one day. More recently, I've thought of translating some Vietnamese poetry with her. I got the idea from working with poet Brenda Hillman on new translations of the Brazilian poet Ana Cristina Cesar, which Hillman began translating with her mother, who is American but grew up in Brazil.

MHK: I think many writers and translators who are the children of immigrants would connect with the anxieties and sensitivities you describe. I certainly do. I enjoy translating from Spanish—a language to which I have no ancestral connection—much more than from Telugu, which is my native language, but not the primary language of my literacy. I have the same sense of failure—in my case a feeling of failing in my first language, failing my origins and culture. Because Telugu is so important to me, and the language already signals a kind of loss in my life, working with it is very fraught. Every attempt at translation from Telugu feels like a repetition of the difficult experience of immigration, whereas I feel quite free when working from Spanish.

I'd love to see what you might do with your mother working from Vietnamese. I have asked my mother to help me at times with translation, and early on I believed that relying on my family for help delegitimized me as a translator. *Kitchen Table Translation* arose in part from my re-evaluation of this notion. It's been great to hear from other writers about how they work with family members. At our first Kitchen Table Translation event in New York in November 2016, Genya Turovskaya spoke about calling her mother from college to ask her about specific words in an Anna Akhmatova poem. And Zohra Saed talked about the back and forth process of working with her father to translate poems from Turkestani. It's not only that I no longer think of such processes as illegitimate, but I also think that working in these ways can expand our understanding of what it means to translate, the way that translation crosses from the literary sphere into life and back.

Given that Brazil and Vietnam are two places that you have a connection to in different ways, have you found any resonances between your experiences of Brazilian Portuguese and Vietnamese? Or if there are not specific resonances, do you access particular experiences or feelings when you leave English (even if you return to it when you actually translate)?

KD: I've thought a lot about how the Brazil-Vietnam connection is somewhat random, and yet I'm always noticing similarities in my experiences with both places. Both are tropical countries, much poorer than the U.S., where a lot of life happens on the streets, in an informal economy. Both nations have a history of hardship and violence that somehow combines with an ability to maintain a certain lightheartedness through suffering and to enjoy just sitting on a stool and watching the world go by, something that Americans don't seem to know how to do very well. I suppose that could be said of a lot of tropical countries.

One convergence that I find more striking is an echo between the languages. Having studied Vietnamese unexpectedly gave me an instinctive understanding of Portuguese spelling and pronunciation, elements that often perplex foreigners. Both Portuguese and Vietnamese have a lot of nasal sounds, and both languages strongly favor open syllables—you never end a word on a closed syllable in either language, even if you see a consonant. For example, "*vão*," which can mean "they go" or "empty space" in Portuguese, sounds just like "*vòng*," which means "round" or "circle" in Vietnamese. The phrase "*đi vòng vòng*," means to go walking or cruising around, so I like to think of "*vão/vòng*" as a place where the two languages I'm closest to intersect.

Imperialism makes for strange bedfellows, and it turns out that the romanized Vietnamese alphabet is derived from the Portuguese because the Portuguese missionaries who came to Vietnam from Macau and Goa in the early 1600s were the first to convert the language from Chinese script into Roman characters. The French Jesuit Alexandre de Rhodes is credited with romanizing Vietnamese, but his 1651 dictionary drew heavily on work done by the Portuguese. So even though there are virtually no Vietnamese in Brazil, there is this unexpected linguistic connection.

In translating Clarice Lispector, I thought about her relationship to Portuguese as the child of immigrants who spoke with an accent and who brought other languages into the home—Yiddish and Hebrew. Lispector clearly dominates the Portuguese language in her writing yet makes these deliberate distortions that I feel must have started from having that window onto other languages that comes with being part of a diasporic community. Having to speak some Vietnamese with my relatives and listening to my mother talk on the phone in Vietnamese for hours definitely gave me a more imaginative relationship to English and to the givens of language in general than I otherwise would have had.

MHK: I think that's something that's not acknowledged widely enough: how access to multiple languages can enhance your imaginative capacities in your primary language.

Lastly, on a slightly different note, what are some works that you love that have come to you through translation?

KD: I can say with conviction that Ferrante Fever is forever for me, and I'll say it five times fast. Elena Ferrante is responsible for making me want to learn Italian next, but I'm also a huge fan of her translator Ann Goldstein, who is now a friend. I discovered the creepy magic of Polish writer Witold Gombrowicz through Danuta Borchardt's intoxicating translations, especially *Cosmos* and *Ferdyderke*. The Senegalese-French writer Marie NDiaye is a more recent revelation. I was completely absorbed by her *Self-Portrait in Green*. I sometimes read books in French, when I'm not feeling lazy, but her translator Jordan Stump does a beautiful job, and it's just a lot easier to get your hands on the translations in the U.S. Yoko Tawada is another writer I'm glad to be able to access through translation. Her *The Bridegroom Was a Dog* was translated from Japanese, and I'm about to start *Memoirs of a Polar Bear*, which she wrote in German and is translated by the highly respected Susan Bernofsky.

Darkness – Translation – Migration

Don Mee Choi

To do your first works over means to reexamine everything. Go back to where you started, or as far back as you can, examine all of it, travel your road again and tell the truth about it. Sing or shout or testify or keep it to yourself: but know whence you came.

—JAMES BALDWIN, from "The Price of the Ticket" in *Baldwin: Collected Essays* (The Library of America, 1998)

I was born in South Korea during the U.S.-backed military dictatorship. I grew up in a small, traditional house my father bought with the award money for his photographs of the Student Revolution of April 19, 1960, which took place in response to President Rhee's anti-democratic and dictatorial rule. What my father still remembers about the uprising is that many children, orphaned during the Korean War, gave up their lives because they had nothing more to lose. What I remember are the children, no older than me, who used to come around late afternoons begging for leftovers, even food that had gone sour. Children with rickets, tuberculosis, and polio were common, and so were the quacks who treated them. The drills at school in preparation for attacks by North Korea kept me anxious at night. I feared separation from my family due to the ever-pending war. I didn't want to end up as an orphan, going from house to house begging for food. I feared what my mother feared—my brother being swept up in protests and getting arrested and tortured. Our radio was turned off at night in case we were suspected of being North Korean sympathizers. At school, former North Korean spies came to give talks on the evil leader of North Korea. I stood at bus stops to see if I could spot any North Korean spies, but all I could see were American GIs. My friends and I waved to them and called them Hello's. In our little courtyard, I skipped rope and played house with my paper dolls amongst big glazed jars of fermented veggies and spicy, pungent pastes. I feared the shadows they cast along the path to the outhouse. Stories of abandoned infant girls always piqued my interest, so I imagined that the abandoned babies might be inside the jars. Whenever I obeyed the shadows, I saw tiny floating arms covered in mold. Mother said mold made things taste better. And whenever it snowed, I made tiny snowmen atop the covers of the jars. Like rats, children can be happy in darkness. But the biggest darkness of all was the midnight curfew. I didn't know the curfew was a curfew till my family escaped from it in 1972 and landed in Hong Kong. That's how big the darkness was.

> . . . darkness is cozy
> Do people know how much it hurts the darkness when you turn the light on in the middle
> of the night? . . . Have you ever turned on the light inside your intestine? . . . When the
> light is switched on inside my darkness, I buzz like a beetle pinned down, bzzz, bzzz,
> bzzz, bzzz, and shake my head wildly . . . The houses with lit windows.
> How painful the light must be for the night.
>
> —**KIM HYESOON**, from "Conservatism of the Rats of Seoul" and "Rat" in *Poor Love Machine* (Action Books, 2016)

> One day I became a halo-child after many days of waving to American Hellos by the roadside with other halo-children . . . We were swell . . . At sunset we parted like tapeworms, breaking off into individual pouches . . . RITZ crackers are impressive too, their enormous holes. Enormity is our savior. We move our heads from side to side, swishing our haloes about . . .
>
> —from my chapbook, *Petite Manifesto* (Vagabond, 2014)

The light ailed us all. Our particular ailment was homesickness. In my new world of Hellos, I swished a halo around my head wildly. My mother's psychosomatic symptoms were frequently triggered, my older brother got called back into the darkness for his mandatory military service, my younger brother had nightmares, sleepwalking almost every night, and my sister excelled in a frenzy, then fell apart, permanently. Nevertheless, life in the light was a privilege. The daily sight of hunger and poverty had vanished overnight. RITZ crackers were no longer a novelty. The crumbs, a mere nuisance. Well-fed, well-clothed, well-schooled, we were swell. Bloated by the light, buzzing. Rainer Werner Fassbinder knows this light all too well. In *Veronica Voss* (film, 1982), the interior of Dr. Katz's clinic is entirely, eerily white except for the so-called "enigmatic African-American GI," rolling cigarettes laced with opiate powder. Here, light is cozy. He's the only shadow in the clinic. He's the new darkness West Germany must numb and sublimate—its post-war hunger and poverty along with its recent past. Let me de-enigmatize the GI's presence in *Veronica Voss* and two other films that make up Fassbinder's BRD (Bundesrepublik Deutschland) Trilogy. The GI signifies U.S. imperialism, allegorically speaking. For me, he's the punctum of the film, to use Barthes' term. He's the new wound. How painful. The meeting of the post-war devastation and systemic racism, impoverishment. When two shadows meet, whether in South Korea or West Germany, a new wound manifests. We try to salve it with opiate or RITZ crackers, but the eternal light, the enormous holes are difficult to plug. Enormity is the price of neocolonial liberation. Raúl Zurita's snow-white smoke laces the sky of New York, the biggest apple of all:

MY GOD IS WOUND

—from *The Country of Planks*, translated by Daniel Borzutzky (Action Books, 2015)

Into the light, thousands of Koreans went, as migrant workers during the 1960s-70s. The workers were granted temporary permits to work as miners and nurses in exchange for foreign aid of 150 million Deutsch Marks. In May 1980, under the tacit consent of the US, the South Korean military carried out a brutal crackdown on the pro-democratic movement in Kwangju. History taught us well. We carried out many massacres during the Korean War. We also massacred Vietnamese civilians during the Vietnam War. We are trained and ready to fight at all times. The US never fails to lead us. In 1983, my family departed once again—this time to West Germany. Into the light, we dispersed, repeatedly—also to Australia and the US. In light, we were to find ways to settle down. In light, we lived like birds.

> Red eyes, sweet cries. My cats that wiggle behind the sofa.
> —from "I'll Call Those Things My Cats" in *Poor Love Machine*

Dr. Katz—she is beautiful. Kim Hyesoon's cats—they are adorable. Kim's darkness is a playground for rabid cuteness in which patriarchy, military dictatorship and censorship, neocolonization and neoliberalism play out. Into this deadly zone, its sky, rivers, and sea, the seventh daughter, the daughter-too-many, enters. She is Princess Abandoned [*Paridegi*/*Parigongju*]. She is the mother of all shamans. Her zone is a zone of wounds, a zone of hysteria, where Barthes' "history is hysterical" also resides. It is *hyŏnbin*. Kim explains *hyŏn* as "closed eyes therefore everything is black" (or blackened by the military censor's ink) and *bin* signifies "a lock, a valley, a mountain spring, a dark womb where the possibility of all life is held, where patriarchy, the male-centered thing breaks."

> The place in which *Paridegi* is abandoned is an unreal place, and all those who raise her are unreal characters. The spaces in which she is abandoned are places where graves are made or where the dead are secretly discarded. Hence, when her foster parents find *Paridegi* as an infant, insects fall out from her eyes, ears, mouth, and nose . . .
> —KIM HYESOON, from *Princess Abandoned*, translated by Don Mee Choi (Tinfish, 2012)

For Kim, in the realm of abandonment, is where, in the pre-modern period, Korean women, blurred the boundary between life and death—"that to live is to die and to die is to live," and, under patriarchy, "that to die is better than to live." For Kim, the overlapping space of life and death, real and unreal, was necessary "in order to express their problematic identities . . . fabricate images of their space and . . . pull out the voices of their transformed selves." This is why, under South Korea's patriarchal-neocolonial-neoliberal rule, Kim "take[s] the readers and stand[s] them in front of the gap of the world, the crevice of death."

> The darkness gives birth, nurtures, and gives birth again . . .
> *Paridegi*'s Buddhist Elysium
> is this black mirror . . . I, a woman poet, on the road of darkness, the endless road of the text . . .
> I break and break apart the darkness I have entered. This is how I can leave here
> and return to the place I had left.
>
> —from *Princess Abandoned*

My encounter with Kim's darkness is what triggered my journey from light back to darkness. Have you ever encountered a mirror like your own in darkness? It "is empty . . . at the very bottom." This is why I say I am a lowly translator. Darkness to darkness, wound to wound, mirror to mirror, translation weaves. Daniel Borzutzky says in his introduction to *The Country of Planks*, "The history of atrocity is not a series of separate events here. Rather, to be alive is to experience all the obliterations at once." The "plains of Nagasaki and Hiroshima" to CHILEAN STADIUM PRISON to PLAYA ANCHA STADIUM PRISON to CAMP PISAGUA PRISON to to VILLA GRIMALDI PRISON to TRES ÁLAMOS PRISON to COLONIA DIGNIDAD PRISON to TRAINING SHIP ESMERALDA PRISON to MAIPO

CARGO SHIP PRISON to CARGO SHIP LEBU PRISON to NAVY BARRACKS PRISON to BERNADO O'HIGGINS MILITARY ACADEMY PRISON to MOCHA ISLAND PRISON to QUIRIQUINA ISLAND PRISON to PUCHUNCAVÍ PRISON to NATIONAL STADIUM PRISON to THOU SHALL NOT KILL, EX. 20:13 to Student Revolution April 1960 to Kwangju May 1980. Translation weaves, it weaves atrocities. And translation mirrors enable us to "experience all the obliterations at once." Rats or planks, they pile up. This is why I say it is painful becoming an immigrant. Depart again, disperse again. This is why I hail, "Migration, my nation!"

> It is a function of poetry to locate those zones inside us
> that would be free,
> and declare them so.
>
> —C. D. WRIGHT

C. D. Wright—she was a force. I felt her force as soon as my future husband at the time gave me a copy of *Cooling Time* (Copper Canyon Press, 2005) and later allowed me to carefully hold his copy of *One Big Self: Prisoners of Louisiana* (Twin Palms, 2003), her collaborative book with photographer Deborah Luster. I met C.D. in person for the first time, two years ago, on my birthday, when Joyelle McSweeney, Forrest Gander, Valerie Mejer Caso, Niina Pollari, and I read our translations at the Red Jewel Box in Seattle. Did you know C.D. was a fierce reader and supporter of translation? Did you know she edited and co-translated *Rain of the Future* (Action Books, 2014) by Valerie Mejer Caso? C.D. was a seer of ghosts. Valerie's poetry is populated by immigrants, family ghosts, their trails of loss, wounds, and violence. That night C.D. playfully demanded that I tell her and Forrest my life story. I told her the story of darkness, the departing, my father filming wars. When I saw C.D. again a few months later in San Francisco, she introduced me to her close friend and said, "Her father filmed the fucking-carpet-bombing in Cambodia." Along the hiking trails at Squaw Valley, which reminded me of the mountains in Korea, we talked about the word Yankee and inter-lingual punning. I used to think that the first syllable in Korean word for American whore—*yanggalbo*—and the first syllable of Yankee, were the same word. Politically, painfully, they are. C.D. got it. She was also a seer of wounds. When I asked her via email for permission to use her line about my father for my book, *Hardly War*, she jokingly said that maybe no one will ask her for quotes after they see this one. No one can anymore. C.D. died in her sleep on January 12, 2016. If we were to follow the logic of Buddhism, C.D.'s soul would have roamed for forty-nine days around March 1. That is when her soul transitions to rebirth, reincarnation. This involves translating her previous life to the next. Fellow Poets, translation weaves, it weaves solidarity.

> don mee—i would love to be a flower—esp if i get to see
> the list and pick my flower
> (I'm particularly fond of country flowers)—later, cd
> (March 12, 2015, 4:11 PM PDT)

swaying hydrangeas
white hydrangeas
rose of sharon
azalea
forsythias
cherry blossoms
declassified flower

Don Mee Choi

UPI flower
classified flowers
baby azalea
blue hydrangeas
merely peony
flower of all flowers
—love, dm

(February 27, 2016 in order of appearance from
"Hardly Opera" in *Hardly War*)

Tomfoolery
by Hilda Hilst

Translated from Portuguese by John Keene

I got tired of readings, concepts, and data. Of being austere and sad as a result. I got tired of seeing frivolities taken seriously and unimaginable cruelties treated with irrelevance, with admiration or utter contempt. I'm old and rich. My name is Leocádia. I decided to drink and screw around before disappearing into the earth, or fire or filth or nothingness. I hired a secretary-companion and said to her: you are young and appealing. When men want to have sex with you tell them to make an effort and sleep with me. I will pay each one of them very well and you will receive princely commissions with each success. She was perplexed. She looked at my still slender but diminished enough figure, asked me to lift my skirt, I lifted it, she looked stunned at my withered thighs. Ma'am, she retorted, it will be very difficult to convince them, but comply I shall, forgive my way of putting that . . . And she ran out of the room toward the bathroom. On returning she told me she had been a teacher and always felt slight nausea when juggling syntax, but before a subject so repugnant (in her view) plus complex syntax, she actually had to vomit. She was red-faced and tearful but proud. She continued: I will behave in an undignified manner to satisfy you so long as my salary is compatible with such awfulness. I told her the amount. She beamed. Her name is

Joyce (!). She is *mignon* and delicious, with a teenager's small breasts, she's 30 but looks 20 (I'm not afraid of syntax), her mouth with slightly raised corners, the light eyes between yellow and brown, hair almost auburn, elegant in gait and posture. Out of nowhere she asked me, in the evening, before my first whiskey (I learned that every drink is less fatal if you start drinking from six o'clock on) if I was familiar with Chesterton. I did not believe what I heard. Was Chesterton some buddy of hers? A teacher? Some politician? No, ma'am, I mean Gilbert Keith Chesterton, English novelist, essayist, critic, and humorist. My God! I exclaimed, I who stopped thinking to continue living, see myself before someone who has read Chesterton. Please Joyce, I warn her, and warn her with a quoted phrase: "If thy head offend thee, cut it off." That's what happened with mine, because for me after all my reflections on the sordidness, the ignominy, the villainy of mankind, I would prefer to forget that a Chesterton existed.

very well, madam, we will not talk about him. would you like to sleep with a man every day?

no way. once per week is fine. on other days I prefer to have a drink by myself, fart, beat my box, and think about trifles.

what?

forget it.

On my fifth whiskey she had understood almost everything. I explained to her that above all the man should be young. That she would make sure of their potency. That she not send me anyone with a nib or a nub. That with me the man remain mute. That I had already arranged a beautiful pillowcase with French lace to slip over my head. She was astonished. I clarified: my wrinkles are sharp enough, I do not want to scare them.

I think, Senhora Leocádia, that you are being too cruel, just too cruel to yourself.

that's none of your business. I know everything about cruelty. I know God.

I showed her a pair of beautiful blue satin pajamas and asked if she liked them. They're beautiful, Senhora, you want to use them next week? They are for you, Joyce, when the young man is at that point send him to me.

perfect, ma'am.

the roll of money will be there.

where?

in my room. order him to look all around him. he will discover it, money sparkles.

Well, now I want to tell you about my son. He is 40 years old. Married. His wife is a bit of an idiot, one of those who talk endlessly and always absurdities. She read someone who was talking about the importance of "speeding up the spoken concept," of gushing. Her visit was hell. I put on my chestnut-colored shawl and sang in a low voice only for her a funny song from my college days: how is it goat beard / it's been a while since we put it in / it's been a while since we fucked ... She completely stood on end. She said to my son: Leocádio, your mother is crazy. how can you leave her here alone when she should be in one of those beautiful places where little old ladies embroider, sing lullabies, fry up dumplings ... you've seen the tools she has under the bed?

what tools?

rakes, shovels, hoes ... and imagine! a tangle of rosaries!

Then I explained with perfect harmony between words that the most sensible thing was keeping tools there because the shed in the back could be targeted by thieves and here in my room only the gardener and Monsignor Ladeira come in.

they come in your room? for what?

the gardener to get the tools and the monsignor to pray.

and he does not have his own rosary?

he does. but he can forget it. and here I have others for us to pray together.

Of course all this was not true. Monsignor Ladeira was a great lover but always forgot his rosary and every week would buy a new one. They sent him to Rome. Pity. The tools were a taurus's fetish. He loved the land so much that he could only achieve pleasure if he had shovels rakes hoes there at the foot of the bed. Disgusted with life he went to be a gardener in a convent. A Wittgenstein type. He had a good schlong. But my son seemed satisfied with those explanations upstairs and told my daughter-in-law the cretin: Leocádia is completely lucid. After having convinced him of my lucidity I hostilely hopped around my daughter-in-law and launching spit in her face I repeated my little song without my son hearing me. Thank God, now they don't bother me any more. Leocádio phones me sometimes. Oh, how delicious and practical it is that people think us strange ... The comfort of no longer being taken seriously, this farting all of a sudden and smiling as if it wasn't you, and being able to caress a dead fish in the fish market and to cry before a scabied and starving dog. It's good to be weird and old. Well. Joyce has been very shrewd. She meets young men and explains everything to them. The first was a very skinny man, sunken chest but a splendid cock, he looked at the money, stroked it, kept it and smiling told me: I'm always at your command, you see, lady? As he was leaving the room I lifted the pillowcase a little and saw his singed pubic hairs and I asked why.

it's because I was making a batch of eggs and oven-baked potatoes there in the boarding house and the oven exploded.

ah ...

does this mean that you talk, lady? and see without seeing?

of course, can't you see?

do you have something else on your face to hide?

just old age.

my grandmother is old and I like her.

but you don't fuck her, do you?

ah, but she doesn't have that much money!

I understand.

He left the room. Suddenly he shouted from the other side of the door: I have a friend who is named Tomfoolery who also has an exceptional piece, can I refer him to Joyce? yes you can, I said. and why is he called Tomfoolery?

a guy wanted give up his ass and a lot of cash to him, and he responded: young ass I eye only and don't put it in. everyone thought it foolish, because with cash people will put it in whatever hole.

of course. yes you can send Tomfoolery.

what do you know, lady. you are a very sensual old lady!

Tomfoolery also is very "sensual," I thought two weeks later, when I got to know him. I'm happy. I even take off the pillowcase.

From Nomenclature, Miigaadiwin, a Forked Tongue

Aja Couchois Duncan

Adze

I should begin with adik, with reindeer and caribou. To know the geography of it, to start with its features.

Your face is this blur of fur and antler.

My story is the history of frontier, a wooded terrain. We could not see each other through the cacophony of trees. But I could hear you breathing. Some kind of wind the nose sings. Adze is stripping the layers off. When the skin is torn from muscle, cleaved from bone.

Agawaatese is not sound but shadow. An interception of light.

Bagijigan

Offering. I have only this. A life without footprints.

From the rooftop anything is possible. Free of ground and its gravities, there is no track of your departure. I found a book of two tongues from which I describe twilight. I too am this in-between thing.

Miziwekamig is not earth. It is adverb; it is strewn about and across. Aki is the name by which the earth is called in secret, what I would have whispered into the soft yield of your belly if you had remained. Now, alone, I could call the world akiiwan, this celestial body. To be gravity and mass, to cling to what you know. I would have given you this, my slippery tongue, but you were walking backward toward the edge of the rooftop. Beyond you was the emptiness of horizon, asphalt, another inanimate future self.

Capital

Dawn is not self referential. Neither is dusk. If I could speak this, if I could, anishinaabe-gaagiigido.

I know only what language makes possible. A tenuous transmission of. I could describe it as inendaagozi or inendaagwad, but meaning is something else entirely. To be remembered is not to hold the idea of oneself, some bundled thing wrapped against the cold.

You once said that nouns were for accumulation, for bartering and trade. Use everything you can, you said. I have laid out all my assets on the rooftop. There is some duplication, an echoing of. In which language should I describe the different parts of me? Inzid, nininj, there is another.

By dusk the buzzards blanket the sky overhead. But my body is less remarkable absent of blood.

I have sorted the dismembered pieces of me according to their function. Appendage is crowded, but indengway has no one beside her. What can one do with a face? Peel back the skin and her features are indistinguishable. Remove nishkiinzigoon and, now sightless, she is without point of view.

Distaff

In old English there is always some German lingering about. I've named the residual Hans and given him a theatrical side. Anishinaabemowin is Maude at the turn of the century. My little bear girl. She is small and dark with a deep guttural laugh. Hans is no match for her.

I begin each day at the spinning wheel. You would call this women's work. But it is Hans whose fingers thread the yarn. Before the end eclipsed the beginning, there was an infinite thread. No one could say where it began and where it ended. No one tied themselves up in little knots.

When Maude wakes she finds Hans with blood-stained fingers. She washes the stains from his niibinaakwaanininjiin, those fragile cups.

Is the story the same without the thread of history? I would ask you, but your past has erased your present. Someone once said that aesthetics are for those without adult responsibilities. Or was it ethics? I always had trouble telling them apart.

Edawayi'ii

There are many ways to tell both sides of it. It is a preposition.

The French mated their way through the colonies. The English claimed only their mirror image. Later the science of alterity would explain such predilections. Absent of Freud, native kinship systems did not distinguish between the progeny of.

Halfbreeds have their own word for gichi-mookomaan, for white person, for butcher knife. Little bear girl took the knife and split herself down the middle. Little bear girl sits beside me on the rooftop, her hair scissoring the wind. Together we watch flora and fauna duck for cover. One is the hydrology of earthquakes, the other less tectonic, more personal. Gichi-mookomaan is nowhere to be found.

It is difficult to be part of a species. There is so little to distinguish yourself from. Sapiens traveled slowly across continents, moved from trees to terra firma. At which point did gichi-mookomaan roam?

They have paved the surface of our habitat, but someday they too will long for the upper canopy. Bipedalism is a fetish of the imperial view.

Feast

In every story of catastrophe, there is a wiikonge which brings the people together. You would call it the ritual of disarmament. But when we met, you hungered for my spleen. The pilgrims hungered for everything. They almost starved.

After the feast, there is always regret. The pilgrims regretted everything they did not steal.

In the spring, when the earth was just beginning itself anew, they renamed it waabooz, a rabbit stripped of its skin. You regretted how you left me, or you should have. I was banajaanh and still nestling.

I've learned that we are all small, insignificant things.

To the wind, there is this fragile expanse of wing. To each other, we are what we do not say aloud, maanadikoshens, horned and reckless.

To be the same is bezhigwan, an inanimate, intransitive thing. I call the world something other than place; I call it bimikawaan. To error is to misread symptom as source. Errors are rampant.

Grammar

No language considers itself part of another. It is not just the eyes or lips or the fault line cleaving muscle from earth, its bone. We are zhiishiib and gookoosh, mammal and bird, between us a separate evolution.

The word for love is similar to the word for spill, for sweeping past the bank. To be married is wiidige, to live together, held by the bows of birch. To be legally married

is something different; it requires a license, an Indian official, things that came later, food rations, theft, disease.

In winter, the warmth of your bed was wiidige, to be hooked around the body of another. The snow was blind to semantic distinctions. The sensation of flushed skin was the same, woman or man, ninaabem or wife. Call it doodooshaaboo and drink.

War in Translation

Lina Mounzer

In the last few months, I've moved houses no less than 35 times.

I have been threatened, beaten, strip-searched, thrown in prison, tortured and made to watch as my mother knelt weeping at the dirty feet of tribal leaders to beg for any information about my kidnapped father. I have waited at countless checkpoints, praying that no one finds the bread, the money, the schoolbooks, the chocolates I have hidden in my bag, on my body, trying to smuggle them through to people on the other side. I have buried seven husbands, three fiancés, fifteen sons and a two-week old daughter I finally agreed to have at 42 for my husband's sake, to bring life back to his tongue after we laid our two grown, handsome sons to rest, one after the other, and grief took all his words away. Our daughter did not die because of a bullet or mortar shell or car bomb, like my father, sister, brother, cousin, mother, neighbor, pharmacist, teacher. She died because the siege had cut off not only our food and electricity, but also our medicine and medical supplies. There were no child-size incubators to be found in our city. My husband rushed her slowly asphyxiating body from one hospital to another until he finally found one in the next town over. He left her with the nurses there and came home at dawn, exhausted but joyful in his relief. In the afternoon he went back to bring her home, and was led away from the small pediatric ward and down to the morgue, where her perfect blue body lay among countless others they had not yet found place enough to bury. Her name was Fatma.

In the last few months, I have watched my city, Maarrat al-Numan, burn, I have watched my city, Raqqa, burn, I have fled Aleppo from the increased fanaticism of the rebels, I have fled Aleppo from the chokehold of the regime, I have fled Aleppo to Turkey, I have fled Aleppo to Lebanon, I have fled Aleppo not knowing if I will ever return, or what I might find if I do.

All this I have watched from my living room in Beirut. Sitting on a worn gray couch with earplugs in, trying to block out the sounds of shearing metal from the construction site right under my window as I translate stories from Arabic to English for the Damascus Bureau, an under-project of the Institute for War and Peace Reporting.

I was tasked with translating mostly those dispatches sent in by women, first-person accounts of life under siege and war, written for the "women's blog" section. Though they are as far from our understanding of "women's blog" in marketing terms as Raqqa now is from Beirut, the degradation and exhaustion of waiting at borders and checkpoints factored into the physical distance.

The women, the writers, range in age from their teens to their sixties and seventies, come from all walks of life, all parts of Syria. They are teachers, activists, seamstresses, farmers, doctors, volunteer paramedics, housewives, writers, aspiring writers, students and revolutionaries.

My body vibrating, whether to the shattering of an earth drill or to the tension of what I read, I have witnessed them march in the streets calling for change, bury loved ones, resuscitate strangers, defy soldiers and snipers, wait in breadlines, pack their whole lives into vans and cars, undergo daily humiliation at checkpoints on their way to and from work, to and from university, which they have refused to leave or discontinue.

To witness, however, feels too passive a word. It is an action that is at its heart, inaction. Their writing is filled with crossings; they are constantly traversing borders both visible and invisible, and it makes me think about the one between these two languages, Arabic and English, each a landscape unto itself. I am also hoping that what I am allowed to smuggle through will survive the journey.

In Arabic, the root of the verb, to witness, is sh-h-d. Roots are important in Arabic. They are present, that is, known and recognizable, not obscure etymologies but immediate and close, giving life directly to all the words that bud and branch from them. From the three-letter root verb, you make the subject and the object, but also adjectives, adverbs and a whole host of other, more complex verbs, subjects and objects related to the first. Even these words—subject, verb, object—are more directly related in Arabic. Translated literally, the subject is the doer, the verb is the doing, the object the one it is done to. In English, a writer writes a book; a letter. In Arabic, *al-katib yaktubu kitab; maktoob.* All from the root *k-t-b*, to write.

From "to witness," we get *shahed*, the one who witnesses; *mashhad*, the spectacle or the scene, but also *shaheed*, martyr; *istishhad*, to be martyred, to die for a cause.

As if the act of bearing witness, followed to the end of one of its branches, snaps under the weight of what is seen, and you fall to your death. As if to die for a cause in Arabic is to bear witness to something until it annihilates the self.

For the last few nights I have been glued to the news, unable to turn it off. Following the progress of the Kurdish forces as they fight the ISIS militants out of Kobane. Over coffees and drinks with friends in our local watering hole in Beirut, we go over headlines, possibilities, projections, trying to keep the quaver of hope out of our voices and words. Unable to allow ourselves to truly believe anymore, after all that we have lived and seen, that a people might be allowed to bear their fates in their own hands without outside interference bending the situation in favor of the hegemonic political agenda. And then it is confirmed: the battle has been won in our favor. The enemy has been driven out of our town. The town council invites us back to reclaim our homes. Immediately I pile into a bus with my mother and sisters for the long journey back to our village, singing and ululating all the way. All I can think of is my journal, with all the poems I have written over the years. Left behind in the rush to leave, I have mourned it every day since, cursing myself for forgetting it. We climb the hill together, a key buried in my mother's pocket, that never once left my mother's pocket, flying the last half kilometer over jagged rocks and dried clumps of earth that were once orchards and fields. I see my mother pull out the key, ready to open the door, only to find a pile of rubble where our house once was. My clothes my journal my needlework our photos shards of our treasured blue cups ground into the dirt. Everything everything gone.

I let out a sob then, breathless with anguish, standing on a hill in Tell Maarouf in a living room in Beirut.

To translate a text is to enter into the most intimate relationship with it possible. It is the translator's body, almost more so than the translator's mind, that is the vessel of transfer. The mind equates words, expressions, deals with techniques and logistics; it is within the body that the real alchemy—mysterious, unnamed and inexplicable—takes place. That alchemy has to do with truth more than signification, that is, the animating force behind signification, which transforms it into meaning, into something that moves. Gayatri Spivak qualifies the act of translation as "erotic," but there is something too gentle about that word to ring true for me. The word captures the act of surrender, and the abundantly physical communion with the text, but there is something messier and bloodier that is elided. More agonized and agonizing too. There is a violence in undoing someone's words and reconstituting them in a vocabulary foreign to them, a vocabulary of your own choosing. There is a violence, too, in the way you are—for long moments—annihilated by the other; undone in return. Neither the translator nor the text emerges from the act unscathed.

I cry a lot while doing this work. It isn't something I can control. Every time I think I have become hardened to these stories, a moment, an expression, a detail will throw me off the scaffolding of language, away from the structural safety of its grammar and rules and headlong into the wilderness beyond. There is always something unexpected, unimagined, no matter how used to the narrative of loss and displacement and violence I think I have become.

When I first receive one of these texts and sit down to read it, I can see her, the writer, clearly in my mind's eye. She gets on the mini-bus. She emerges from a taxi. She calls the neighbors, asking when they last saw her brother. I am aware that this first-person voice is hers, and of how it conjures her up as vividly as the images she shows me through her eyes. And then I sit down to work, taking in her words, her voice, anew. And two contradictory things become true at once:

despite the fact that I am attempting to reproduce her words as faithfully as I can, they must now re-emerge in words unavoidably my own. And *because* of the fact that I am attempting to reproduce her voice as faithfully as I can, it must now re-emerge in a voice unavoidably my own.

"I get on the mini-bus," I write. "I emerge from the taxi," and then it is I calling the neighbors, and I am nearly hysterical with worry as I wait for their response. In the considered, deliberate act of translation, these I's bump up into one another again and again until they are accidentally shattered, the various pieces of these commingled selves becoming, for long moments, indistinguishable from one another. Afterward, trying to pick them up and separate them out, I am left with a thousand cuts I can feel every time I move or breathe. Afterward I realize that there is a shard I have failed to remove, that it has entered my eyes and become lodged there, cutting into my vision always, digging into the form and content of my memories.

Translation is not just about transposing words from one language to another. But transplanting a feeling, a way of seeing the world, from one vocabulary of experience to another. I think of the verb, *to transplant.* A seedling from soil to soil. But also an organ from body to body. The procedure must be as delicate, as cognizant of the original conditions of creation in order to nurture and ensure a continuation of life.

In Arabic, the word for the action of transplantation is *zare'*. Simply to plant. There is no prefix implying movement from one place to another, an in-built warning of possible rejection. There is only the thing itself, planted, as if the process of its life begins all at once in this new soil, this new body. I prefer this way of thinking about translated words, and the possibility of their finding life. But the conditions of growth, for growth, remain the same. There are still no guarantees that anything will take root, or that the new body will not reject the new organ for being foreign.

When my family and I washed up in Canada, carried out on the great wave of migration away from the civil war in Beirut, I found that I could no longer unlock the trunk in which I carried the words to explain where I had come from, what I had lived. When I did manage to force it open, what I found inside was soggy, useless. The words were all in another language, non-native to this new soil. I translated them as best as I could. *Qazeefeh* became shell. *Msalaheen* became militiamen, gunmen. *Hajez* became checkpoint. *Malja'* became shelter. But the new words were strangely light. They carried none of the weight of what they truly meant. *Qazeefeh* was piercing and hot, abject terror, near-misses and direct hits. It was luck and unluck, it was what left the neighbor boy with melted clumps for hands and took away my grandmother's hearing in one ear and what missed my father again and again as he crossed the border to Syria and back over four long years, on his way to the Canadian consulate, checking on the status of our visas. *Msalaheen* were those who held your life in their hands every time you passed through a *hajez* made of sandbags, militia flags and insignia fluttering above, the colors and shapes meaning the difference between friendly and unfriendly, sometimes life and death. *Msalaheen* scrutinized your papers and peered into the car with slitted, predatory eyes as you made yourself as small as possible, trying to pretend you couldn't smell the stink of your parents' fear. They were those who kept your neighborhood safe; those who made your neighborhood a target. *Malja'* was long sleepless nights, the whole building crowded into one airless underground room, the dizzying smells of mold and other people's bodies, listening to *qazeefeh* after *qazeefeh* fall all around you, the echoes booming in your chest as intimate and sure as heartbeat. But *malja'* was also endless games of cards and forced sleepovers with friends caught at your place overnight, watching the way the old neighbor twitched as he snored and plotting to steal his dentures while he slept, your giggles luckily muffled by the sound of gunfire. Gunfire now the catch-all name for M16, Kalashnikov, 120, B7, Grad, Doshka, Katyusha, 155, Hawen; my skill in telling them apart by sound now rendered useless.

But once I had the words translated, I found that no one really wanted to hear them, be near them. They were light in English, yes, but also cumbersome and huge. Giant styrofoam shapes. When I carried them with me into the classroom or into the home of new friends, I had to struggle to fit them through the door. Their size dwarfed me, crowded me out; everyone stared. When I tried to put them down, they formed a barrier, setting me apart as so inconceivably other it became impossible to clamber over them, to find my way back to the world of school dances and mall outings, pop quizzes and notes passed back and forth about your crush this week.

In order to enter, then, to become one amongst the many individuals that made up my new world, I had to let go of that whole lexicon, repudiate it, as if it were a sort of shame.

For years I wrote stories about Jennies and Alexes and Melissas, about their suburban childhoods and private disappointments, about dreams and desires moved only by the eddies of a personal history, floating far above the undertow and tidal shifts of collective history. Trying to rewrite my past in an effort to not have to translate it.

I had become used to feeling light. I did not want my country hanging around my neck like a weight I must always carry; unable to take it off or put it down. I did not want to be buffeted about in the whirlpool resultant from the violent meeting of two currents, the personal and the historical, perpetually sucked down into the eye of the vortex along with the thousands upon thousands of other bodies carried there by the same riptide. And everyone around me drowning-how could I live with attempting to save myself alone?

It goes the other way, too. I remember how a student in one of my creative writing classes once handed in a story set in Beirut, about a college student like him pining over a girl who then rejected him in favor of another, richer and more muscular. A story he told us was based on personal experience. His characters were called Damien, Samantha and Brad. Not entirely unheard of here, but odd enough as a group to raise an eyebrow. While workshopping his story with the class, I asked him why he had not named them Salim or Dala or Bilal. His name, after all, was as Arab as they come.

"But Miss," he replied, incredulous. "I'm not writing about war and bombs and tragedy. Why would I give them such names?"

A bomb is a shocking experience. Even to one who feels they have become inured to it. Each heart-hollowing concussion is a redefinition of everything you ever thought you understood. It has nothing to do with fear. Fear is something you get used to, it becomes the new baseline from which your body operates. Quivering, animal, alert. You even come, in the dark *malja*' of your consciousness, to accept the idea of your own death. But the breathless outrage of being reduced to utter insignificance—each bomb a punctuation of this idea—is not something you ever get used to. For it is not merely your interiority that is threatened with annihilation, but the entire surrounding world that grounds it in meaning. Parks, schools, streets, friends. Squares, alleys, journals, children. Rivers, parents, trees. Husbands, wives, orchards. Snatches of celebration and joy. Moments of silence and repose. The cat curled up on the garden wall. Stacks of old photographs, your grandmother standing ramrod-stiff for the cameraman in the first flush of her youth. The paintings carefully chosen and framed on the wall. The plants in powdered milk cans all in a row, their leaves tangled into one canopy. A brown egg on a blue plate one early morning. All the people, places and things of your life that you have stacked and shored up against nothingness, all flattened into a grainy, featureless landscape to the inhuman scope from above. All of them collateral damage.

English is the *lingua franca* of the media, and regardless of what I know of poetry or fiction, which has room enough to embrace foreignness, to break the audience-pleasing structure of introduction-crisis-resolution, I am aware always of the prevailing narrative of the media, because it is there that we, who are not of the predominant culture but who write in its language, who feel ourselves always implicated in two worlds, read about ourselves most. We know how language can be used to beat the rhythm of the war drum, mustering ranks upon ranks of public support. We know how language itself can wage war against us, by mimicking the same casual dehumanization of a bomb. Everyone you know and love: terrorists. Militants. Strategic targets. Collateral damage. The leveling of your neighborhood: an unfortunate mistake. The razing of your city: the birth pangs of a new Middle East. Seven dead, twenty wounded. Forty-one dead, ninety-three wounded. 1.2 million refugees. 2,000 migrants.

All the life squeezed out of them so that they fit into one headline. Sentences become coffins too small to contain all the multitudes of grief.

The trauma, recreated in words: countless particularities flattened and rubbled into one. In the mediatized narrative, your individuality, your personhood, is not a right you are granted by virtue of being human. To become a story worthy of unfolding in the small confines of the mass media, you must earn your individuality by lifting yourself up and out of collective circumstance, either by the exceptionalism of your life or the spectacle of your death. For the story to come to an end, you must serve the purpose of the story, not the other way around. As such, lessons are learned; resolutions are reached; audiences are comforted.

But there is no real resolution to the trauma of the collective. It lives on in all the stories you will ever tell from now on, in all the stories that will be passed down along the line of culture, even when they are about something else. It reshapes your vocabulary. It becomes part of your language. A *barrel* will no longer ever be a barrel again; shrapnel will always explode from it. The word *mustard* will forevermore carry a whiff of gas, rashing your skin, smarting your eyes. When you say *Sabra*, or *Shatila*, you are not referring to a place, but to a heap of dead bodies shot indiscriminately and tossed aside like worn rags. When you say the word *catastrophe*, no one need ever ask which one it is you mean. It is towns, cities in their entirety become past tense. These are things that can only ever be reproduced, retold, re-imagined, but never, never laid to rest or resolved. There is no end to the story, only the story.

When writing about war, I am often at a loss as to how to proceed. I want to make the writing as dissonant as I can, to recreate a sense of disruption, of an essential brokenness. I want to make the writing as unobtrusive as I can, to have it slip easily into the mind, mild-mannered and unassuming, before revealing that it has been wearing a vest of explosives all along. But these are theoretical questions, questions of technique, and ultimately ways of distancing myself somehow from a raw wound at the core that simply and only begs to be told, no matter how.

But told to whom? Who is the reader I'm addressing when I am writing in English? It is not my mother tongue, though I feel almost at home in it, though I love it as if it were my own. Like any language, I know it is a tool, as available to raw beauty as it is to hegemonic violence. And I know the only way to redeem it for all of us who it marginalizes is to fight our way out of those margins and insist on being part of the text. But my English is a war wound. It is a result of the roughshod amputation of my mother tongue. Because we were forced, or rather, allowed the privilege to flee at an age when I was first learning to use my voice on the page. But it is a wound from a war much older than that. Because even before we left, I read mostly in English, I was encouraged to read mostly in English, I was complimented on my English, I was told, in a thousand different ways, that it was superior to Arabic, more accomplished, more intelligent, more likely to be taken seriously. It has taken me a long time to allow myself permission to use it as I wish, to break it and retake it without the secret childhood hope that the highest compliment that should be paid to my writing is that I sound like a native speaker.

And I wonder, what is it that brings me to the page? What brings me back, again and again, to the war? To the site of that wound and the need to try and make sense of it through language? Is it the desire to know or the desire to be known?

Now I am back inside my childhood, in the world of *malja'* and *qazeefeh* and *msalaheen*. Stopping at *hajez* after *hajez*. Learning the names of the many *hawajez* that strike fear into the heart of the Syrians. The same way Hajez el Berbara was notorious among some Lebanese—spoken of like a dread portal with its own metaphysical logic, either allowing you through and past or swallowing you up and disappearing you—the Syrians have Hajez el Muqass, Hajez el-Conserwa, Hajez al-Khanaser and countless, countless others. These were once names of common places, squares or streets or bridges crossed without a second thought, now made otherworldly borders with that prelude. The word itself a portal into the uncanny.

I stop at these checkpoints every time with my heart carried in my mouth like contraband that might be dropped or crushed or lost at any moment, knowing I will pass through, because there is a story on the other side of that *hajez*, but not knowing in what shape; not knowing what distortions that portal might work upon my body.

I often wonder, while working, if I should add an asterisk, an explanation, context, use those translator's tools at my disposal to broaden the world beyond the page. To drive home a certain urgency; to explain how everyday objects become sinister or meaningless or numinous during wartime.

Windows. Clocks. Mirrors.

A Note on the Translation: war changes the laws of physics, bending time and space to its will.

Sometimes I do add notes, small parenthetical asides that are no real elucidations at all, for words I am familiar with but whose permutations accumulate, and other, new words, their meaning created and destroyed in the same moment by the explosion of violence.

Hisbah, for example. Qualified as (ISIS religious police), other times as (ISIS morality police). Does the word strike the same fear in your heart as it does mine, reader; does it elicit the same disgust that such flesh-hungry men might dare invoke the name of God and his morals, the God I have spent my whole life serving in my heart and dressing modestly for? Does it ignite the same incandescent rage as I watch these blasphemers from Libya, Tunisia, Saudi Arabia, Lebanon, Egypt, Pakistan and sometimes Europe and America, snatch *my* revolution, my revolution from my hands and use it to whip my back? I, who was willing to alienate myself from my family to print pamphlets and distribute them, organize rallies and advise people on the best way to run from tear gas and live bullets, defying even the men in my cell who said that revolution is no place for women?

Shabbiha, for example. Sometimes left as is, but italicized, since they are so common to the landscape of the Syrian war, predating as they do the Syrian war. Sometimes qualified as (secret police), others as (regime thugs or collaborators). Have I described them well enough that you understand, reader, how they are a monstrous thing that haunts and shadows, even though I cannot explain the aural recall of the word *shabah*, ghost? How they are the hellhounds of Bashar al-Assad, willing to rip your life apart for whatever scraps their master throws their way? How they are one of the reasons we revolted, and that shucking our fear of them to march in the streets with heads held high and sure was the first revolution we enacted upon ourselves?

When I tell you of how I smuggled in fancy chocolates and trendy shoes through the checkpoints at a risk to my life, are you disappointed in us for not being pristine in our victimhood, or must I add a note to explain how even in siege people might prioritize luxury over necessity to live as opposed to merely survive?

When you hear me exclaim, over and over, *"Alhamdulillah!"*—"Praise God!"—when I hear that my son or husband has been killed by a sniper or car bomb or left gutted on the side of the road by the *shabbiha* (though we now use the word *martyred* for all the war dead, including two-week old daughters who die because of a siege on medical supplies), do you think me so twisted into barbarism by my baffling religion that I might truly find joy in this news, or must I add a note to explain that submitting to God's will is the only way I have not to go utterly mad with grief fighting it?

When I tell you how my nine-year-old cousin was martyred his first day fighting on the frontlines, do you think us monstrous to have let him go, or must I add a note to explain how we have come to accept that in war the desire to fight and its attendant risk of death is something that doesn't respect childhood?

You understand at least that merely lifting my voice to tell you these things is an act of trust, of faith in your ability to understand. And that I, as a translator, must if nothing else respect and reproduce the faith inherent in those words. To excise my paranoia about the English-language reader's judgment from all my work. In that way, I am learning too that even as I speak of death and destruction, my every word becomes a force shored up against them as soon as it is written.

Often I imagine these women one day waking up and realizing that this is it. The end of this chapter. One day they open their eyes after blinking away a sleepless night spent worrying over the future minutes, the future years, and decide that whatever gamble they will be taking to leave is better than the gamble of staying. And so, in the quiet dawn of a room, in the midnight roar of barrels falling from the sky, they pack up what they cannot imagine leaving behind. They gather their children close and call their husbands, they pick up elderly parents and arrange whatever bundles they have made, that they are able to make, tight. They leave in droves or as single families, they leave in worn-out slippers, in trendy, sparkling heels, on bare feet, leaning on canes, clutching infants to their breasts. They leave behind their houses, their streets, their cities, their countries, their dead. And they set off out into the unknown, carrying the memory of all that they leave behind in their hearts and on their tongues, even if they carry nothing else. These they will resurrect in stories, and these stories will be passed on, and so they will endure. This is what they carry, this is what they bear. They are bearing their witness.

And we who listen to their stories are also bearing witness. Carrying something whose significance cannot be described in language, but must nevertheless be contained within it.

A journalist friend tells me about being in Greece, reporting on the arrival of refugees in Lesvos, rising from the sea both resurrected and, like Lazarus, irrevocably transformed by death. On the backs of the trucks circling the town is the word "*metaphoros*." A Greek acquaintance explains that this means transport, and she is struck by this, as I am too when she tells me about it. How going back to the roots of language can reveal something essential about a word's purpose. How stories might be transformed and disguised to pass through the world more easily, but still smuggle with them the same truth. And how the perfect metaphor for the acts of reading and writing, and the witness you must bear to perform each, is translation, specifically its Latin root: to cross, to carry over. For they all require an active form of engagement that is at once, paradoxically, an active form of surrender. You must bear the words, no matter how heavy or foreign or grotesque or strange, you must bear them with their full weight and allow them to carry you where they will, carry you so far into yourself you finally emerge into an understanding beyond. Beyond the self, beyond language. A place where you might, for endless moments, imagine that you have become someone else entirely, and thus emerge transformed, bearing back with you into the world the knowledge that such a place exists, that such metamorphosis is possible. I am not entirely sure how one does this. There are no maps to these territories that lie beyond the borders of that which is explicitly voiced. But I do know that the only way to evaluate what must be carried over and how, what can be sacrificed or modified and what at all costs must not be lost, is to journey across that border.

Translation is a symbiotic act. Between writer and translator, of course, but also between languages. In becoming its vessel, you carry over something of yourself but also something of the original language, because that is the way that language works. It is a communal heritage, but is also something entirely individual, entirely your own. And that is what gives it its transformative possibility: this inevitable commingling of self and other, of self and culture, of personal history and collective history. Language gives the individual the power and strength of the collective. And writing, speaking, telling stories—wielding language in narrative form—has the ability to transform the collective through the individual experience. To cross over from that which is felt, experienced, to that which is voiced—for the purpose of witness and being witnessed—is each and every time the declaration of a singular understanding of what it means to be alive in the world. This opens up new spaces, new imagined possibilities, and those, through language, become part of the collective heritage.

It is the best form of resistance I can imagine for a world scarred with forbidding, categorical borders. Between the self and other, between where you come from and where you end up, between the personal narrative and collective history, between genders and cultures and languages and countries and the similar calls for dignity and recognition contained in stories. The only way to make borders meaningless is to keep insisting on crossing them: like a refugee, without papers, without waiting to be given permission, without regard for what might be waiting on the other side. For when you cross a border, you are not only affirming its permeability, but also changing the landscape on both sides. You cross carrying what you can carry, you cross bearing your witness, you cross knowing that you are damageable, that you are mortal and finite, but that language is memory, and memory lives on.

Istishhad: to be martyred; to die for a cause.

It is an especially difficult word to translate, because it has been so marred by blood and violence, so disfigured by zealotry and malice. It is a word that has been ripped from its roots, those that connect it to something so emblematic of what it means to be human, to be driven always by the twin desires of wishing to know and wishing to be known.

Its root: sh-h-d, witness. In its most literal form, *istishhad* in fact means: to have been witnessed. Witnessed by God, who is nothing, symbolically, if not the omniscient reader—and writer—of the human condition. To be witnessed is what gives one's life meaning; that is what gives death its cause.

And yet, despite all this, there are times when I am wrung out. When I wonder if there can be any consolation in the exulting of our collective ability to use language to heal and bridge and repair in the face of such violent ruptures of meaning. What is the use of such abstract consolation in the face of the hard, physical realities of hunger, of fear, of being forced to flee home, of being unable to flee home, of being a teenage girl who goes down to the cellar to get her pyjamas and is then caught on the landing by a hail of sniper bullets as her father and I watch helplessly from above, unable to pull her out of harm's way?

"In a few minutes," she writes, "the bullets stopped falling and my father came down and carried me into the house. Two bullets had pierced my foot and I had shrapnel wounds all over my body. When I saw all the faces around me and all their falling tears, I tried to console them.

'Don't cry,' I said. 'I'm alive, alive, alive.'"

Four Poems by Cecilia Vicuña

Translated from Spanish by
Rosa Alcalá

La Gitana Dormida
(Un león vigila su cuaderno de sueños)

La Gitana ha escrito durante años
una obra secreta que nadie jamás
conocerá, pero que ha empezado
a realizarse en la vida real.

Mientras ella continúa soñando
sus sueños forman el mundo.

El león, sin embargo,
no puede dormir.
Si deja de vigilarla,
ella podría despertar
y nosotros desaparecer
instantáneamente.

The Sleeping Gypsy
(A Lion Guards Her Dream Journal)

The Gypsy has been writing for many years
a secret text no one will ever
read, but which has begun
to materialize in real life.

While she continues dreaming
her dreams create the world.

The lion, however,
cannot sleep.
If he ceases to watch her,
she could awaken
and we vanish
instantly.

Horticultura

Durante épocas enteras
me cultivé a mí misma
como un demonio sin freno
y hoy me veo
con freno de mano
como niña de mano
deforme y delgada
en un jardín
de plantas de humo.

marzo 1972

Horticulture

For ages
I cultivated myself
as a freewheeling devil
and now here I am
a handmaiden
with a handbrake
diminished and deformed
in a garden
filled with plants of smoke.

March 1972

Cecilia Vicuña Ramírez Lagarrigue etc.

Cecilia del latín
"la que no ve"
Vicuña del euskara
"tierra baja"
Lagarrigue de la garriga
"formación vegetal"
del vasco francés
y Ramírez
patronímico de antiguo
hijo de Ramiro
Mezcla de reyes con idiotas
hidalguía y vulgo
mierda y barro.

junio 1971

Cecilia Vicuña Ramírez Lagarrigue etc.

Cecilia from the Latin
"she who cannot see"
Vicuña from the Euskara
"lowland"
Lagarrigue from garrigue
"vegetal formation"
from the French Basque
and Ramírez
ancient patronym
son of Ramiro
Mixture of kings and idiots
nobility and commoner
shit and mud.

June 1971

Lo Casual

La idea de encontrar lo casual como algo
que estaba cuidadosamente preparado
por una mano anterior que encadenó
sus formas estéticamente
para explicar un jardín desordenado
que está en el punto preciso de su desorden,
un gesto sin consumar, que se agita levemente
sin que se sepa qué va a ser de él.

La indeterminación, la musicalidad
del movimiento de algunas hierbas
abandonadas a sí mismas
doradas de sequedad
a causa de una emoción
que sufrió su dueña
que antes se ocupaba
tan tiernamente del alelí
y ahora ha dejado
que todo crezca
y solo visita el jardín
para dejarlo languidecer.
Azaroso y muelle
todo se ha cansado
y vive por casualidad.

29 agosto 1970

Chance Encounter

The idea of coming upon the unexpected
as something carefully arranged
by a prior hand that linked
all its forms aesthetically
to explain a disordered garden
at the height of its disorder,
a gesture not yet carried out, gently stirring
with no way of knowing what will become of it.

Indeterminacy, the musical
sway of certain grasses
left to fend for themselves
brown and parched
consequence of an emotion
the owner suffered
she who so lovingly tended
to the wallflowers
and now has let them
grow wild
who visits the garden
only to let it languish.
Precarious, given to its fate,
all has become weary
and by chance lives.

29 August 1970

The Dark Girl's Laughter

by Vimala

Translated from Telugu by Madhu H. Kaza & Sitaramayya Ari

The Chennai train station was not very crowded at that hour. As I pulled my heavy suitcase onto platform number seven, I heard a woman laughing. I was reminded of Madhuravani's laughter in the movie, *Kanyasulkam*. Before me was a tall, slim girl in a chudidaar, her wavy hair clipped to her head. She had big black eyes, a straight nose, a dimple on her right cheek and pearl-white teeth. For a second I stood there looking at the black-skinned girl although the Kachiguda Express was already in the station.

On the train I found my berth, stowed my luggage and settled into my seat to read William A. Jackson's *Tyagaraja: Life and Lyrics*, which I had purchased in Madhurai. Though the book was interesting, I found the small print irritating. I looked up to see the girl on the platform talking to a man about 60 years old and holding his hand in hers. At the last moment, the girl boarded with a suitcase and two bags and landed on the seat opposite mine. She continued talking with the man through the window. They spoke in Tamil. As the train began to move, the girl stowed her luggage, began texting and made some phone calls, whispering in Telugu. She looked like one of those girls who work for a software company. I got involved in my book, and the girl made another phone call speaking as if she were pleading for something.

During the day the humidity had been unbearable in Chennai. By the time our train reached the outskirts of the city it had started raining. I closed my book and watched the huge drops fall. The wind blew the water into the compartment, so we had to close the windows. Some water still leaked through the window frame. I removed my luggage from under my seat, put it on the overhead rack and said to the girl, "Your luggage may get wet, too."

"The water won't come this far," she said. She pulled a thermos out of her bag and asked, "Would you like some coffee?"

Warm coffee in the rain! "It's very good," I told her as I sipped from the small steel cup she'd given me.

"Appa makes great coffee. I told him I didn't need it, but knowing that I like it, he brought some anyway."

The girl hadn't checked her seat number when she boarded, so I asked, "Do you have a reservation?"

"No, this is an unexpected trip. I couldn't get a reservation. And the general compartment is impossible."

"Ask the ticket collector. You may still get a berth," I offered.

As soon as the ticket collector appeared, she and four other passengers swarmed around him asking for berths. They followed him down the compartment. Eventually the girl came back disappointed.

"I never get on a train without a reservation. Usually I take the Charminar Express. This is my first time travelling without a reservation," she said.

"What will you do now?" I asked.

"Well, I'll lie down here. If anybody comes and claims the berth, I'll just get up and spread my blanket on the floor."

Where would a girl who never travelled without a reservation get such an idea?

The rain stopped, and I opened the window. Drops of water

continued to drip from the crossbars. I looked out at the wet greenery and felt a pleasant breeze. Daylight was fading into twilight. Our train passed through a village. Five or six children, barely clothed, stood at a distance and waved at the train. I waved back.

The girl's eyes were closed and she was crossing herself in prayer. When she opened them, she looked at me and unfurled a smile like a blossoming flower. Her face was mesmerizing. She pulled out two hardcover books from her bag. After leafing through the pages she put one of them away and started writing intently in the other. Her phone rang, but the call was dropped before she could answer. She tried calling the number, but apparently her phone was dead. She asked me to keep an eye on her luggage and walked to the other end of the compartment to charge her phone.

The train entered Andhra.

The girl started writing in her book again but not as quickly as before. She appeared contemplative, looking out the window now and again. I had often seen fellow passengers reading books intently but never writing like this.

"Do you like reading?" she asked.

I smiled and nodded, "Yes."

"Are you from Chennai?"

I shook my head.

"Where are you from then?"

"I am from Hyderabad. I was in Madhurai for work and now I'm going home."

"I don't know English. I haven't studied much, just up to tenth class in my village. And in a Tamil language school."

"But you speak Telugu so well—I thought you were Telugu," I said.

"Well, I can't read or write Telugu, but I worked hard to learn how to speak it," she said.

"Your Telugu is good."

"Isn't it? That's because I have been living in Hyderabad for ten years!"

"Do you write poetry or stories?"

"Oh no! Why did you ask that?" she asked.

"Well, you have been writing for a while now." I smiled.

"Oh, that! It's my diary. It's a habit from my childhood. I was at Appa's place the last few days and didn't have a chance to write."

At Renigunta a few men entered our section of the compartment. The girl had to give up her seat and stand. I signaled to her to sit next to me and she did.

"What's your name?" she asked.

I replied and asked for hers.

"Madhurima," she said.

I told her it was a lovely name. She smiled her beautiful smile. Her phone rang again, and she answered, speaking in Tamil for a while.

It was a night of the full moon. I always love watching the moon on those nights when it slips behind clouds and peeks out again. But the view disappeared as the train made a turn along the tracks. The girl still had her diary open in her lap and appeared to be deep in thought. Who knows what she was recollecting that brought a tear down her cheek. I looked away so I wouldn't disturb her.

The railway staff were filing up and down the compartment calling out numbers and handing out meal packages. It was then that she asked, "Shall we have dinner, too?"

I placed a bookmark in my book and opened the package of pongal I had purchased at Saravanam. The girl opened a packet of idlis wrapped in a banana leaf. The pongal was made with ghee and cashew nuts but there was no more than about six spoonfuls of it. I shared it with the girl.

"Appa makes good coconut chutney. Not just coconut chutney, he makes everything well," she said, offering me some of her idlis and chutney. She was right; the idlis were very good.

"What about your mother?" I asked.

"My mother passed away when I was little. My sister is sixteen years older than me and raised me like a mother. My brother-in-law works as a clerk at the government college in Villupuram. As a child I lived there for a few years.

When I asked what she did, she laughed. "Oh, odd jobs, nothing much."

Her phone rang again. Just as she began talking, the call was cut off. Mumbling that the battery was going dead, she got up and went to the end of our compartment and plugged her phone into the charging unit. An hour later she was still standing there talking on the phone. I spread a blanket on my lower berth, arranged my traveler's cushion as a pillow, put my reading glasses in their case, sipped some water and lay down under another blanket. I must have been tired; I fell asleep right away.

I was awoken at about two in the morning by screams. At first I didn't understand what was going on. Turning the light on, I realized that the girl had probably slept on the floor between the berths. She was now sitting and screaming at the old man lying on the berth on the other side. He was also saying something to her.

"What's going on?" I asked.

"You know I didn't get a berth. It's tough traveling in the general compartment, particularly at night, so I spread my blanket here on the floor and slept. This old guy, he put his hand on my chest. I thought maybe his hand slipped down by accident, so I pushed it back to the berth. Twice. But he's a pervert. He did it again and again." Turning to the old man she said, "You probably have grandchildren my age—you still don't have any sense? You look like a gentleman on the outside. What the hell do you think you are doing?"

The man didn't take it quietly. He began to insult her. Infuriated, I got involved and scolded him. A couple of other passengers got involved, too. Then the woman on the middle berth got down and exchanged berths with the old man. By the morning, he was gone.

As I washed my face and dried off with a towel, the girl handed me a cup of a hot brew. I didn't usually drink tea or coffee on the train because the colorless, tasteless stuff disgusts me. But I accepted her offer.

"Thank you, madam," the girl said to the woman now seated on the opposite berth. "If you weren't here last night who knows what else the old guy would have said. We should never trust the ones who look like gentlemen. It's not that bad with rowdies because they actually look like thugs, and we can be on our guard."

Her phone rang again, and again the call got cut off.

"Could I please use your phone?," she asked, "Mine's been giving me trouble since yesterday, and I have to make an urgent call." I gave her my phone but it didn't help. Apparently the signal strength was poor at our location. She sprinted to the end of our compartment to charge her phone, stood there for a while and talked very fast. I opened my book again, but it was difficult to read the small print, so I pulled out *Frontline* from my bag and started reading an essay from where I had left off.

The girl came back and sat next to me. The train was running late, and she was anxious. Her phone rang again. "I am almost there. It shouldn't take more than an hour and a half. I will definitely be there. Please look out for me," she was saying to someone.

The train moved slowly, stopping and starting. It finally came to a halt about thirty kilometers from Hyderabad. When I asked the ticket collector why the train had stopped, he said that there had been an accident and that the track was being repaired.

"Are you going to be late for something?" I asked the girl.

"Yes, madam. I got some work after trying for six months. If I lose this opportunity it's going to be hard." She paused and said, " I went through a lot the last six months." I didn't say anything. She continued, "I have to be at Ramoji Film City at nine. First I need to get home to Krishnanagar, freshen up and then rush over. It is already six thirty. I don't know if I can get there even if I hail an auto."

"What do you do?" I asked.

Her face brightened. "I'm a dancer. I do group dances in movies. Also in programs for television."

She asked me if I had watched a certain television serial. I said I didn't watch serials. I didn't even own a television set. She was surprised.

This young girl, who didn't look quite twenty-five, must have had a lot of hopes riding on this opportunity.

"Do you want to become a star?" I asked.

She laughed out loud. Her laughter revealed a dimple in her cheeks and narrowed her eyes. The white stone in her nose stick sparkled. She was truly pretty, that dark girl.

"Me! A star! Who would take me? I am a mother of two. How old do you think I am? I turned thirty one just recently!"

It was my turn to be surprised.

"In fact I wanted to become a dancer—I learned Bharatanatyam for four years. I don't like the stuff in movies, all that jumping around that they call dance, but that's what's keeping me fed. Appa used to work as an assistant to a stunt master. After my mother passed away he left me with my sister. He didn't marry again. He loves me and my sister dearly. Unfortunately, he broke his hip bone one day while working on a movie.

"Appa had no other skills. By that time, I had passed tenth grade, with excellent scores, but given the circumstances, I had to move to Chennai to cook and care for Appa. I couldn't continue with school; instead I worked as a salesgirl in a big mall. Appa's colleagues asked him to get me into the film industry, but I wasn't interested. Neither was Appa."

"But then, how did you get into it?" I asked.

"Well, not everything is in our hands, is it?" she laughed. "Folks say that our fates are scripted well ahead of time. Maybe that is how it happened."

The train moved a little, then stopped again.

Her phone rang. "I am looking for a ride. I'll let you know as soon as I find one," she said to whomever had called. Then she turned to me and said, "Let him wait. If I tell him I am still on the train, he will take somebody else."

"Maybe life would have been different if I had not met Subrahmanyam," she said.

"Subrahmanyam?"

"He was my husband."

"What happened to him?"

"That bastard, he gave me two children and then one day suddenly he remembered his father, his mother and his caste and ran away. He left me and married a girl of his own caste."

"I was naïve in those days, just sixteen, seventeen years old. He was very fond of me. He worked as an accountant in a company. He was eight or nine years older than me. Appa and my sister didn't approve of our marriage, so we eloped to Tirupathi. Then we went to see his folks but they didn't want to have anything to do with us. We stayed in the homes of friends for a while, and finally he found a job in Bangalore, where we lived for about three years. It was there that our daughter was born. We didn't have anybody in Bangalore to help me during that difficult time. My family came after we asked them for help. They yelled at me. They cried. My sister took me to her home in Villupuram. I stayed with her for about three months until my health recovered and then returned to Bangalore.

"What I didn't know at the time—Subrahmanyam didn't tell

me—but I learned from others later, was that Subrahmanyam's older brother and father visited him while I was at my sister's. After that I noticed a gradual change in his behavior. He would get angry with me for no reason and belittle my family and my caste. He wouldn't talk to me. I didn't know what to do. I used to cry a lot, but I'd put on a smile for him when he came home from work so he wouldn't know how I felt. That was at least what I thought."

It was just past 7:30. A little boy entered the compartment with a basket and called out, "Hot, hot samosa!" They were the really small Hyderabadi samosas. He gave me twenty of them for ten rupees. I spread them on a paper between the girl and me and offered to share them. She continued talking: "By then I was pregnant again; my daughter wasn't even a year and a half. My health was pretty bad. My sister came and stayed with me for a couple of months. Subrahmanyam said that he had found a good job in Hyderabad. He would go, find a place and then he would come get me. He left, but he never answered my calls after that. I had no idea where he was working in Hyderabad. His colleagues from his old office had no idea either. Finally one day he called me and said that he, in fact, hadn't gotten a job at all and that I should vacate the house in Bangalore and take my daughter to my sister's. He would come get me after he found a job. I didn't know what to do. My brother-in-law came to help me pack up and we all went to my sister's place in Villupuram. I was seven months pregnant at the time. Appa was distraught. That was the last phone call from Subrahmanyam. I gave birth to a baby boy."

"What are your children like?" I asked. "They must be like you."

"Well, their father is from a higher caste, so they are fair-skinned. My looks and his color. But how will they turn out? Who knows! If they don't become rascals like their father I will be happy."

"So, did Subrahmanyam eventually come to get you from your sister's place?"

"Even if he came, how could he be my husband? The guy who disappeared on me never showed up again. But I saw him again about four years later on a railway platform. He was holding a child in his arms and there was a woman standing next to him, probably his new wife. As soon as he saw me, he jumped onto the train, came out from the other side and ran off. Bastard!" she laughed.

"With two children, it must have been . . . "

"Yes. With two little kids . . . by then I was twenty or twenty one. Where would I search for Subrahmanyam? His family lived in Chennai, somewhere in Mambalam. I had no idea exactly where. I had gone there just once, right after our wedding. But I was turned away back then, wasn't allowed even to enter the house. Anyway, with great difficulty my brother-in-law found the address and we all went there: me, my sister, my brother-in-law, Appa and my two kids. His folks made a big scene and threatened to call the police on trespassing charges if we didn't leave immediately. My brother-in-law is a gentle creature. Appa doesn't know much. He is uneducated. And we didn't have anybody on our side for support. So that was it. After that I left my daughter with my sister and came with my son to live with Appa. I had to find a way to stand on my own two legs and I was done with Subrahmanyam. That bastard! When I think of those days, my blood boils. I did odd jobs including washing dishes in people's homes. Appa opened a small stall at home to sell cigarettes and candies and cared for my son.

"It was then that Appa's friends asked me again if I would be interested in working in the movies. Appa was against it, but I said I would do it if the work was outside Chennai. That was how I came to Hyderabad with Appa's friend, Uncle Ramdas."

"To become an actress?"

"No, just to make a living. I didn't care what type of work I did. I had to feed my kids and support Appa. Those days I found small roles in films. I lived in a small room in Uncle Ramdas's house. As you know people working in films and destitutes like me, we are prey to everybody."

Her eyes glistened with tears.

"You can't escape some things," she said, smiling with wet eyes. I understood what must have happened.

"There were so many times when I wanted to leave Hyderabad and go back home. But I can't do this type of work back there. I feel very sad sometimes thinking about my situation. I write when I feel sad or happy. I write everything. Appa bought me a diary for my birthday the year I passed tenth grade. He said, "If your mother were alive you would tell her everything. Think of it like a mother and write everything in it."

"Some days I didn't find time to write, so there would be blank pages in the diary. Now I use a bound notebook and write on the days that I can. And I read my stuff whenever I get time—pain and sadness in some pages and happiness in others."

"You were writing last night. Was it happiness?" I asked.

"Yes. I saw my children in Chennai. I stayed with Appa for a few days. Of course I was happy. And it rained! The wet, green trees; the rain water sliding down glass windows. Don't you find the rain beautiful!" She laughed like a little girl.

"Yes." I said. "You said you write everything. You don't worry about someone reading your journal?"

"Well, I change names. And I write in Tamil. I've filled fourteen notebooks so far, all in Tamil. Nobody knows Tamil where I live, not even Sreenu."

"Sreenu?"

"He works as an extra in movies. We live together now. So far he's been good. The only problem is he drinks. But then I drink, too, once in a while." She laughed.

"If you both are playing small roles, isn't it difficult to manage when you don't have work?" I asked.

"Well, sometimes there are plenty of opportunities. A while ago I was working a lot for television. In fact I saved a bit and purchased a housing plot in Villupuram. I would love to return to my village someday. My village is about thirty kilometers from Villupuram. I remember living there with my grandma. I have lots of memories: the farmlands, the tamarind trees, the river where we swam. I was friends with a lot of boys. We used to lie down on a bed of thatch on the river bank and tell each other stories as we watched formations of flying cranes."

Meanwhile her phone rang again. "Well, not much . . . there's a huge traffic jam here in Afjalganj . . . looks like there was an accident ahead somewhere. What? I can't hear you." She hung up.

"Why did you lie?" I laughed.

"I don't know what else to do. The film shoot is at twelve. We're supposed to be at the studio by nine. This scene was supposed to have been shot about ten days ago. It was postponed. I thought I had some time, so I went home to Tamil Nadu, but they called me up to return immediately. I can't afford to miss this shoot."

"Why don't you get off the train right here and go. Isn't it closer from here?"

"Yes. But my costumes are in my room. I just can't show up without them."

Another two hours passed. She continued telling stories about traffic jams over the phone. Just as the train was nearing the Kachiguda station the girl asked me if I knew anybody who worked in television. I said I didn't.

She pulled her suitcase and bag from under the seat, threw the backpack on her shoulder and wrapped her chunni around her head a couple of times so that her face was all covered except for her eyes. She tied the ends of the chunni at the back of her head and put on her glasses and started to roll her luggage towards the door of our compartment. As soon as the train stopped, she jumped down to the platform.

I quickly tore out a page from my notebook, wrote down my name and phone number on it and called out, "Madhurima!"

She came back to the window and said, "Sorry I didn't say goodbye. I'm worried about being late."

"I imagine your traffic jam should last at least an hour and a half more," I teased. "If you ever feel like giving me a call, please don't hesitate."

She laughed and hurried away. The piece of paper I gave her—I saw it fall out of her hand.

As I was collecting my luggage I found her journal on a nearby seat. I grabbed it and hurried to the platform to look for her. I knew it would be difficult to find her. I didn't know what to do.

In the auto on my way home I opened the journal. It contained four hundred pages of writing in a steady, beautiful, Tamil hand. There was an inscription on the first page—Mani, Care of Rangarajan—followed by an address in Chennai.

At home I showered and brewed a hot cup of coffee. Then I went to the office and fell back into my work routine. The following Sunday, I found a little time to catch up with the pile of old newspapers and magazines that had collected in my absence. It was then I noticed her journal again. What should I do with it? Where would I find the girl? The paper on which I had given her my name and phone number had fallen out of her hand. It occurred to me then that she might have deliberately discarded it. Maybe we can talk most freely with people we are unlikely to meet again.

Between the pages of the journal there was a photo of two children, ten or twelve years old, standing next to an old man, who looked like the Appa who was with Madhurima in the train station at Chennai.

I thought of throwing the journal away. But remembering how dear it was to the girl I thought of mailing it to the address on the first page. If Mani was Madhurima, the journal would reach her. If not? Well, what would happen? Whoever received it would not be able to read the other thirteen books anyway. As I turned the pages in the journal, I noticed some places where the writing was stained. Tears probably. Between some pages there were dried rose petals, jasmines and a peacock feather.

I could still hear the dark girl's laughter.

"Somos los del español deficiente": Crip Chicana/ Filipina Pedagogies of Translation

Sony Coráñez Bolton

Translate, queerly

"Los poemas de Federico García Lorca / The poems of Federico García Lorca," one student declared on the first day of my course "Comparative Borderlands: The Feminist and Queer Cultural Politics of Filipina/o and Latina/o Diasporas." By way of introduction, especially as an Asian American Studies trained scholar now teaching in the Spanish and Portuguese Department at Middlebury College, I was curious as to which cultural texts partially or even wholly convinced my students to pursue Spanish language studies. The way I phrased it was thusly (translated from my Spanish, of course): "When were you like 'Ok, this is it; I'm all in. I'm learning this language.'" One student pleased and surprised me by passionately declaring his love for the love poems of Lorca. And while Lorca's queerness is an uneasy topic for some in the canonical machinations of the Generation of '27's inclusion into an Iberian cultural archive, queer love for Lorca's queer love poetry still emblematized a geopolitical exclusion at the heart of Hispanic Studies that "Comparative Borderlands" seeks to amend.

"Raise your hand if you knew that the Philippines was a Spanish colony for over three hundred years / Levanten la mano si sabían que las Filipinas fue una colonia española por más de tres siglos."

"I wonder how many of you know that the Philippines was once a US colony/¿Cuántos de Uds. sabrán que las Filipinas fue una vez una colonia estadounidense?"

I wrote Lorca's name on the whiteboard in front of the classroom alongside other foundational figures in Hispanic letters: García Márquez, Paz, Borges, Ortega y Gassett, Martí, among others. A seemingly wide geographic spread, students noted the very gendered orientation of the collaborative list, a list that was the fount of *their* inspiration to pursue Spanish. I turned my students' attention to what our collective inspiration said about Hispanic Studies as a field. This is certainly not a new critique. The patchwork of national traditions that compose Hispanophone literatures is decidedly and unavoidably gendered. While pure, our collective inspiration results in an inevitable masculinism—indeed, the Spanish language could be put to different ends, but what got us there in the first place was a rendering of linguistic mastery (or, at least the desire for it) and literary value that proliferates what queer theorist Michael Warner called "regimes of the normal."[1] I hoped to reframe this heteronormative proliferation of Spanish *belles lettres* and "queer" it for more just ends—a queering that emphasized the merits of the comparative and the interstitial nature of the border. This begged a geopolitical question about the organization of knowledge of the Hispanic. Indeed, it was not just about who we imagine as Spanish words lift from our lips, but also where we imagine the "Hispanic" even happens.

While *who* is certainly a perennial question of import in a class on the dialectics of human movement, nation, identity, and diaspora, the questions of *where* and *which* are the national projects of literary excellence we are asked to apprehend was also prioritized. Which cultural archives are so marginal that translating them would not even be entertained as a thinkable possibility? Whose subjectivities could never even aspire to the coherence of the nation and instead had to make due with broken, garbled disarray? When we looked at the whiteboard we observed the conventionally constructed projection of the "global Hispanic," a necessarily messy and clunky umbrella term; it amalgamates traditions of cultural production across space and time. However, where the Philippines is concerned it does so without complete regard to precisely where Spanish imperialism traveled. Spain's far-flung Asian colony too oriental for consideration. For my pedagogical purposes, a glaring yet under-remarked linguistic reality of the Philippines remains a seductive explanation for exclusion from Spanish and Latin American canons and pedagogies meant to cultivate mastery of the language of Cervantes: the Philippines is not Hispanophone and I, a Hispanophone Filipino, am teaching a class on Spanish Filipino writing. As pedagogical praxis, the linguistic incapacity of the Filipino to speak the language of its erstwhile colonial masters inspires my turn to a crip translation of Chicana feminism.

Crip Chicana Translation and the Filipina Postmodern

Responding to similar colonial legacies twinning the Spanish-American imperial projects, Jessica Hagedorn's *Dogeaters* presents an important, if problematic, vista of the ways that Hispanicity obtains in Filipino cultural production. Teaching *Dogeaters* in its original language directed attention to other ways that the Philippine Hispanic emerged in the texts: references to Catholicism, the elitism of a Filipino upper class, the lexicographical and morphological affinities between Tagalog and Spanish, etc. I assigned a "Traducción crítica" [Critical Translation] of individually selected passages from *Dogeaters* meant to consolidate and put into practice the knowledge students gained from an extended unit on US and Spanish colonialism in the Philippines. In fact, this was the one primary source text that I taught in English. Jessica Hagedorn's *Dogeaters*, a canonical postmodern Filipino American novel morphed into something else as it was translated to Latina/o Studies. My students were to select a passage from *Dogeaters* and translate it from English into Spanish. To introduce the project, I instructed students to provide an "ensayo de justificación" or justifying essay where they wrote about their process, their strategy, and the difficulties of the project. What surprised me was the Latino and Latina heritage learners of Spanish and their approach. They convinced me in many ways of Hispanic Asias being a vital site of Latina/o cultural politics, which was the point of the course all along (The Philippines was colonized by Spain for over 300 years yet has not received much critical attention in Spanish Departments).

Beyond giving students a rigorous expansion of their vocabulary, the assignment required them to synthesize meaning across a large body of text. Most importantly, they had to be attuned to the historical and socio-political contexts in which *Dogeaters* circulated vis-à-vis overlapping and sequential colonial projects. One student, for instance, elected to include more gender inclusive language in her translation, aligning herself with the Latinx movement. Inspired by Gloria Anzaldúa's epiphany of hearing the feminine plural "nosotras" for the first time, she claimed that there can be and there should be feminist translators and that we should perform feminist translations. While this might seem counterintuitive for some translators, this problematized language mastery in the enterprise of translation. Pedagogically, it is important that we impart on students that translation is an interpretative endeavor, an act of intimate close reading. Once more, when translation is performed along the backdrop of compromised archival access, it's important not to praise the translator's ability to rectify the fact of inaccessibility. Rather it's crucial to contextualize translation as a response to the historical, social, and political circumstances that renders certain archives opaque and how those same circumstances linguistically endow particular readers the capacity and gift of access. This partly comes out of a commitment to disability critique and its transnational application to cultural and linguistic sites in which difference necessarily obtains differently.

Disability Studies was foundational to the pedagogical approach to translation that I endeavored to rationalize in my course. This might not be new to many readers, nevertheless, it became necessary to engage translation not as an empirical practice that gobbled linguistic inputs to generate atomistic and interchangeable outputs. This imagines a monolithic cognitive profile able to engage and manipulate discourse. There is a subject of translation endowed with a cognitive capacity to make language fungible. This is disrupted by the fact that two authors (or translators or artists?) given the same texts will not produce identical translations. This reality questions the interchangeability of translated documents. The translation is filtration—words are filtered through a body, an identity, a time and a place. Embracing this inherent infungibility, translation then becomes a form of interpretation, an intimate form of close-reading (maybe the most intimate) or a "work of art" per Walter Benjamin.[2] Additionally, the realities of the Filipino archive set up, at least for me, a painful backdrop through which we pursued Hispanic Philippine culture: the Philippines possesses a rich Spanish language archive of writing produced by Filipinos, which is largely inaccessible to Filipinos today. In a Spanish course my job is to teach Spanish but what does that mean when the linguistic home of a constellation of texts is not its geographic home? What does it mean to translate texts for a population to which those texts actually belong?

I refused approaches that would thematize the historical incapacity of the Filipino to access their past Hispanic heritage as a "lack" to be "fixed." Such an approach would be tantamount to a "colonial model of disability" characterizing an entire population unfit to engage their own intellectual and cultural patrimony.[3] Instead, I turned to Chicana feminist theory's embrace of polyvocality, hybrid being, multiple Spanishes, and *mestiza consciousness* to understand the ironies that inhere in the Filipino archive. Toward this end, part of the purpose of this pedagogy think-piece is to understand Anzaldúa's feminist re-articulation of the border vis-à-vis disability studies; I argue that we achieve this re-articulation through a comparative Filipina/Latina border critique. In a foundational piece of writing that has enormous implications for the teaching of translation, Anzaldúa lists, in order of power, the various kinds of Spanishes that populate what we might call the "Hispanic." Before this though she gives us an impassioned argument for maintenance of the integrity of Chicano Spanish:

> "Chicano Spanish sprang out of the Chicanos' need to identify ourselves as a distinct people. We needed a language with which we could communicate with ourselves, a secret language. For some of us, language is a homeland closer than the Southwest—for many Chicanos live in the Midwest and the East. And because we are a complex and heterogeneous people we speak many languages. Some of the languages we speak are:
>
> 1. Standard English
> 2. Working class and slang English
> 3. Standard Spanish
> 4. Standard Mexican Spanish
> 5. North Mexican Spanish dialect

6. Chicano Spanish (Texas, New Mexico, Arizona and California have regional variations)
7. Tex-Mex
8. *Pachuco* (called *caló*)"[4]

Anzaldúa defines English distortions of Spanish as *pochismos*. What about Spanish distorted by Tagalog or other Philippine languages due to contacts between Filipino peoples and Spanish colonists during Spain's 333-year stay?[5] Anzaldúa continues and offers the insightful disability-adjacent formulation of hybrid language and identity stating that she and others like her are "*Deslenguadas. Somos los del español deficient*." That is, we are "the obscene. We are those of deficient Spanish."[6] In affirming deficiency and multivariant Spanishes, Anzaldúa proposes a queer language politics of preservation against hegemonic standardization. Anzaldúa defiantly refuses the empiricism of translation and articulates a "mestiza consciousness" through the mixed poetics of Chicana Spanish. When I say that Anzaldúa refuses the empiricism of translation, I mean that she refuses the logics of a coherent and monolithic sign system wedded either to Castilian Spanish or US English. This holds value for a course given in a Spanish department, whose overall pedagogical goal is linguistic proficiency or mastery. We trouble what "mastery" means in the Borderlands. In this way, the Borderlands of Anzaldúa's queer of color and feminist cartography is translatable to the Philippines. This holds special meaning for translation pedagogies—we must be careful that in eliciting understandability from student translation that we aren't propelling the normativizing of language. However, it's crucial to recognize that the type of queer linguistic preservation that Anzaldúa proposes is not possible for Filipinos, the lost "Latinos of Asia."[7] Nevertheless, the Chicana feminist Borderlands remain a pliant and useful metaphorical space that I find pedagogically inclusive of other forms of Asian Hispanicity that may fall beneath the radar in more conventional understandings of Hispanic national literatures and cultures. Part of understanding this is embracing the deficient and non-deficit based pedagogies of translation.

1. Michael Warner, *Fear of a Queer Planet: Queer Politics and Social Theory* (Minneapolis: University of Minnesota Press, 1993), xxvii.
2. Walter Benjamin, "The Task of the Translator," *The Translation Studies Reader*, ed. Lawrence Venuti (London: Routledge, 2000).
3. The "social model of disability" might be familiar to many readers. Proponents of this model argue that bodily variation or incapacity do not inherently signify disability. When the body interacts with a social, political, and economic environment then incapacity translates to disability. This resists a "medical model of disability" which treats disability as a lack of normal functioning to be corrected without regard to the social environments that make impairments difficult to manage. Thus, disability becomes a social issue rather than an individual problem.
4. Gloria Anzaldúa, *Borderlands/La Frontera: the new mestiza* (San Francisco: Aunt Lute Books, 2012). 55.
5. Ferdinand Magellan first "discovered" the Philippines in 1521. However, the first Spanish settlement in the Philippines was established in 1565.
6. Ibid., 58.
7. Anthony Ocampo, *The Latinos of Asia: How Filipino Americans Break the Rules of Race* (Palo Alto: Stanford University Press, 2016).

The Desert Survival Series/ La serie de la sobrevivencia del desierto* (excerpt)

Various Translators

Amy Sara Carroll
Francheska Alers-Rojas
Julieta Aranda
Elizabeth Barrios
Iván Chaar-López
Orquídea Morales
Omar Pimienta
and
Mary Renda (Spanish)
Mona Kareem (Arabic)
Bruna Dantas Lobato
(Brazilian Portuguese)
Eleni Stecopoulos and Irene
Stecopoulos (Greek)
Wen Liu (Taiwanese
Mandarin)
Shahnaz Habib (Malayalam)

* The Desert Survival Series/La serie de la sobrevivencia del desierto was written as a group of 24 poems that were included in the Transborder Immigrant Tool, a project of the Electronic Disturbance Theater, a collaboration between Micha Cárdenas, Amy Sara Carroll, Ricardo Dominguez, Elle Mehrmand and Brett Stalbaum. The Transborder Immigrant Tool was designed as an app for flip-phones that could help migrants cross the desert between Mexico and the U.S. more safely. Carroll notes, "this series serves as a direct response to the US government's post-1994 conversion of the Sonoran Desert into an agent of border enforcement."

1.

The desert is an ecosystem with a logic of sustainability, of orientation, unique unto itself. For example, if the barrel cactus—known otherwise as the compass cactus—stockpiles moisture, it also affords direction. As clear as an arrow or a constellation, it leans south. Orient yourself by this mainstay or by flowering plants that, growing toward the sun, face south in the Northern Hemisphere.

El desierto es un ecosistema único en si mismo, con su propia lógica de sustentabilidad y orientación. Por ejemplo, el cactus de barril o biznaga—conocido como cactus brújula—acumula el rocío y la humedad, también proporciona direcciones. Tan claro como una flecha o una constelación, se inclina hacia el sur. Oriéntese haciendo uso de este recurso o por las plantas que florecen, creciendo hacia al sol, ya que éstas siempre apuntan hacia el sur en el Hemisferio Norte.

ةمادتسالا نم ديرف قطنم ىلع شيعت ةيئيب ةموظنم ءارحصلا
بونجلا يف ةفورعملا صيصألا تارابص تناك اذإف .لالدتسالاو
لالدتسالا انل نكمملا نمف ،ةلصوبملا تارابصلاب (اكيرمأ نم) يبرغلا
لثم ةخماش فقت نهنم ةدحاولاف.ىشطعلا اندولج اهب بطرن امدعب اهب
شطع ورا وأ اهرثأ عبتت .بونجلا هاجتا يف نيلت امنيب ،ةبكوك وأ مهس
،ضرألا دسج يلامشلا فصنلا نمو ،سمشلا هاجتاب ربكت يتلا راهزألا
.بونجلا وحن كهجوب علطت

2.

Climb or walk in the morning. Rest midday beneath creosote bush or mesquite, insulating yourself from the superheated ground. Remember—even the sidewinder hovercrafts, the bulk of its body above the scalding sand as it leaves its trademark J-shaped tracks across the desert dunes.

Camine o escale en las mañanas. Descanse al mediodia bajo un mezquite, una hediondilla o gobernadora para protegerse de la abrasadora temperatura del suelo. Recuerde—aun la víbora de cascabel aerodesliza la mayor parte de su cuerpo sobre la ardiente arena mientras deja su característica huella en forma de "J" a lo largo de las dunas del desierto.

Caminhe ou escale de manhã. Descanse ao meio dia debaixo de um arbusto de creosote ou mesquite, se protegendo do solo muito quente. Não esqueça—até mesmo a cascavel-chifruda flutua, a maior parte do seu corpo acima da areia escaldante, deixando seu típico rastro em forma de J pelas dunas do deserto.

3.

Just before sunrise, Bedouins turned over half-buried stones in the desert to catch the dew that the night's coolness had condensed on the stones' surfaces. Indigenous travelers in the Mexican-U.S. corridor searched the broad leaves of yucca and agave. Rainwater collected at each plant's base—the leaves' apex—remaining there up to a few days after a summer or winter shower. Proceed from the simple premise: The desert caches water in unlikely places that it resists divulging. Do not expend all your energies searching for its secret stashes, but likewise do not assume that its pockets of moisture are nonexistent. Restrict your water reconnaissance to early or late in the day when your liquid net-gain will outweigh the perspiration you expend. A thirst is seldom quenched; it morphs to reappear on the horizon. Meanwhile, the desert reflects the sun back like a mirror. You are caught in that pair's uneven, inconsummate exchange.

Justo antes del amanecer, los beduinos volteaban piedras semienterradas para atrapar el rocío que el frío de la noche había condensado en su superficie. Los viajeros indígenas en el corredor de México-Estados Unidos buscan las anchas hojas de la yuca y el agave para abastecerse de agua. El agua de la lluvia se acumula en la base de cada planta—el ápice de las hojas—permaneciendo ahí hasta unos días después de una llovizna veraniega o invernal. La premisa a seguir es simple: el desierto acumula agua en lugares inesperados que resiste divulgar. No agote sus energías buscando sus escondites secretos, pero igualmente no presuma que sus bolsillos de humedad son inexistentes. Limite su búsqueda de agua al principio y al final del día de manera que el líquido que encuentre sea más que el sudor que transpire al buscarlo. La sed es rara vez saciada: se transforma para reaparecer en el horizonte. Mientras tanto, el desierto refleja el sol como en un espejo. Usted está atrapad@ en el medio de este intercambio desigual e inconsumado.

8.

According to Herodotus, King Cambyses, twenty-five hundred years ago, lost his entire Persian army (fifty thousand men) in an Egyptian sandstorm. Deserts guard their secrets; no archaeological evidence corroborates Herodotus's account. Sudden, local haboobs—sometimes the result of thunderstorms' cool air outflows—still menace desert travelers. Instruments in the Mojave Desert have clocked wind speeds up to one hundred sixty kilometers per hour. In a sand or dust storm, heat suffocates; winds transubstantiate the landscape into unidentified flying objects. Sand becomes sandpaper against the skin. Turn your back to the wind. Lie on your side against a hill or dune. Wrap your face. Cover your nose and mouth. Tuck your eyeglasses into your shirt or jacket pocket (so the wind will not etch its soliloquies into them). Wait it out. No Godot, a sandstorm will go the way of a temper tantrum.

Según Heródoto, el rey Cambises perdió todo su ejército persa (cincuenta mil hombres) en una tormenta de arena egipcia hace dos mil quinientos años. Los desiertos guardan sus secretos; no hay evidencia arqueológica que corrobore la versión de Heródoto. Repentinos haboobs locales—a veces el resultado de las corrientes de aire frío generadas por las tormentas eléctricas—todavía amenazan a los viajeros del desierto. Los instrumentos en el desierto de Mojave han registrado velocidades de viento de hasta ciento sesenta kilómetros por hora. En una tormenta de arena o polvo, el calor sofoca; los vientos transubstancian el paisaje en objetos voladores no identificados. La arena se convierte en papel de lija contra la piel. De la espalda al viento. Acuéstese de costado contra un cerro o duna. Cubra su cara. Tápese la nariz y la boca. Guarde sus lentes en su camisa o en el bolsillo de la chaqueta (para que el viento no grabe sus soliloquios en ellos). Espere a que pase. Ningún Godot, una tormenta de arena seguirá el camino de un berrinche.

16.

An antioxidant, an anti-inflammatory medication, the ubiquitous creosote bush rejuvenates itself via a cloning process. With a life span upwards of 9,000 years, it is esteemed by the Tohono O'odham to be the oldest living thing on earth. Ten years after a 1962 Nevada thermonuclear explosion destroyed twenty-one creosote bushes, twenty re-sprouted as if to protest, "We will not be moved." *Hiroshima mon amour*—no ghosts, no burns, no shadows. The creosote bush simply grows—a survival artist.

Un antioxidante, un medicamento antiinflamatorio, el ubicuo arbusto de la creosota se rejuvenece a través de un proceso de clonación. Puede vivir hasta 9,000 años y los Tohono O'odham pensaban que era el ser viviente más antiguo de la tierra. Diez años después que la explosión termonuclear de 1962 destruyó veintiún arbustos de la creosota en Nevada, otros veinte retoñaron casi en forma de protesta. "No nos moverán." *Hiroshima mon amour*—sin fantasmas, sin quemaduras, sin sombras. El arbusto de creosota simplemente crece—un artista de la sobrevivencia.

Ένα αντιοξειδωτικό, ένα αντιφλεγμονώδες φάρμακο, το πανταχού παρών κρεόζωτο θαμνώδες ανανεώνεται μέσω μίας διαδικασίας κλωνοποίησης. Με μιά διάρκεια ζωής πάνω από 9.000 χρόνια, έχει εκτιμηθεί από τους Tohono O'odham ότι είναι το αρχαιότερο πλάσμα στη γη. Δέκα χρόνια μετά την θερμοπυρηνική έκρηξη του 1962 στην Νεβάδα που κατέστρεψε είκοσι θαμνώδη κρεόζωτα, είκοσι ξαναφύτρωσαν σαν να διαμαρτυρηθούν, "Εμείς δεν θα μετακινηθούμε." Hiroshima mon amour—δίχως φαντάσματα, δίχως εγκαύματα, δίχως σκιές. Το κρεόζωτο θαμνώδες απλώς μεγαλώνει—ένας καλλιτέχνης επιβίωσης.

20.

Do not panic. Do not panic. If you are too tired or disoriented to continue, realize that you probably will not be thinking clearly. Heat scrambles the brain like eggs. "It is perfectly noble to come out of a pose." Know your own limitations. Turn your phone on. Search for a signal. (Walk only if you are not in range. Then, power the phone down to save the battery life to save your own. Walk, retest. Walk, retest, until you secure reception.) Call 9-1-1 or 0-6-6. Reason—it's better to live to cross the desert tomorrow than to let the desert cross you today.

No entre en pánico. No entre en pánico. Si está demasiad@ cansad@ o desorientad@ para continuar, dese cuente que probablemente no va a estar pensando claramente. El calor revuelve el cerebro como huevos. "Es completamente noble salir de una pose". Reconozca sus propias limitaciones. Prenda su teléfono. Busque una señal. (Camine sólo si no está dentro de la cobertura. Luego, apague el teléfono para conservar la vida de la batería para salvar la suya. Camine, repita. Camine, repita, hasta que encuentre señal.) Llame al 9-1-1 o 0-6-6. Razone—es mejor vivir para cruzar el desierto mañana que dejar que el desierto le crucifique hoy.

別驚慌。別驚慌。如果你累了或暈了，不能再繼續下去，無法清晰思考。熱流攪和腦汁像　蛋液。「放下姿態完全是一個高雅的表現。」了解自己的極限。打開你的手機。尋找訊號。（往前走，若你不在訊號範圍內。接著，關上你的手機以節省電池壽命，及連帶著的你的　性命。往前走，重新測試，直到你確保了訊號。）播號給9-1-1 或0-6-6。原因—若能活 到明天去穿越沙漠，總比讓沙漠在今日穿越過你好多了。

22.

Ultimately, many would argue that nature sets the standard for neutrality. Unlike human beings, nature maintains no allegiances to nation, family, business, religion. You already know that the greatest danger you face in the desert may not be the climate or the terrain. Some will not have your best interests in mind. Rescue workers pledge to offer assistance to those in need; hold them to that promise. Trust no one else who's a stranger with your life.

Al fin y al cabo, muchos argumentarían que la naturaleza establece el estándar de neutralidad. A diferencia de los seres humanos, la naturaleza no mantiene lealtades a una nación, familia, negocio, religión. Usted ya sabe que el peligro más grande al que se enfrenta en el desierto no es necesariamente el clima o el terreno. Algunos no tendrán su mejor interés en mente. Los rescatistas se comprometen a asistir a los que necesiten ayuda; aténgalos a cumplir esa promesa. No le confíe su vida a ningun@ otr@ extrañ@.

23.

When everything—including this cell phone—fails, build a signal fire in dirt or sand, away from brush and trees. Use dead cacti and mesquite. A fire in the shape of an "X"—the international symbol of distress—needs no translation.

Cuando todo—incluyendo este teléfono móvil—falle, construya una señal de fuego en la tierra o en la arena, lejos de arbustos y árboles. Use cactus muertos y mezquite. Un fuego en forma de "X"—el símbolo internacional de peligro—no necesita traducción.

എല്ലാം -- ഈ സെൽഫോണുൾപ്പടെ എല്ലാം -- പരാജയപ്പെടുമ്പോൾ, മണ്ണിലോ മണലിലോ തീയുണ്ടാക്കുക. ഉണങ്ങിയ കള്ളിമുള്ച്ചെടികളോ മെസ്ക്വിറ്റുകളോ ഇതിനായി ഉപയോഗിക്കാം. ഇംഗ്ലീഷിലെ X അക്ഷരത്തിന്റെ ആകൃതിയിൽ വേണം തീ ഉണ്ടാക്കാൻ. അത് സഹായഭ്യര്ഥനക്കുള്ള അന്താരാഷ്ട്ര ചിഹ്നമാണ്. തർജമ ആവശ്യമില്ല.

Contributors

Rosa Alcalá was born in Paterson, New Jersey, to Spanish immigrants. Alcalá is the author of three books of poetry: *Undocumentaries* and *The Lust of Unsentimental Waters*, both from Shearsman Books (2010 & 2011), and *M(y)Other Tongue* (forthcoming 2017, Futurepoem Books), and is the recipient of an NEA Translation Fellowship. *Spit Temple: The Selected Performances of Cecilia Vicuña* (Ugly Duckling Presse, 2012), which she edited, was runner-up for a PEN Award for Poetry in Translation. She lives in El Paso, Texas, where she teaches in the Department of Creative Writing and Bilingual MFA Program at the University of Texas–El Paso.

Francheska Alers-Rojas is currently a PhD student in Developmental Psychology at the University of Michigan.

Julieta Aranda is a conceptual artist that lives and works in Berlin and New York City.

Sitaramayya Ari has written short stories in Telugu and translated Telugu fiction into English. He lives in Michigan and teaches biochemistry at Oakland University.

Elizabeth Barrios immigrated from Venezuela to Illinois at the age of twelve, where she lived until beginning her graduate studies at the University of Michigan in 2009.

Sony Coráñez Bolton received a PhD in American Culture and Ethnic Studies from the University of Michigan, Ann Arbor. Sony is a 2016–2017 C3 Mellon Postdoctoral Fellow at Middlebury College. In the Fall 2017, Sony will teach in the Department of Spanish and Portuguese at the University of Arizona as an Assistant Professor of Latin American Cultural Studies.

Amy Sara Carroll, Assistant Professor of American Culture, Latina/o Studies, and English at the University of Michigan, is the author of two collections of poetry *SECESSION* (Hyperbole Books, an imprint of San Diego State University Press, 2012) and *FANNIE + FREDDIE/ The Sentimentality of Post-9/11 Pornography* (Fordham University Press, 2013) and the monograph *REMEX: Toward an Art History of the NAFTA Era* (The University of Texas Press, forthcoming). Since 2008, she also has been a member of the collective Electronic Disturbance Theater 2.0/b.a.n.g. lab, co-producing the Transborder Immigrant Tool, which was included in the 2010 California Biennial. Recently, she was named a 2017–2018 fellow at Cornell University's Society for the Humanities.

Iván Chaar-López is a PhD student in American Culture at the University of Michigan.

Youmna Chlala is an artist and a writer born in Beirut and currently based in New York. Her book of poetry, *The Paper Camera*, is forthcoming from Litmus Press. She is the founding editor of *Eleven Eleven {1111} Journal of Literature and Art.* Her writing appears in publications such as *Guernica*, *Prairie Schooner* and the *MIT Journal* *for Middle Eastern Studies*. She has exhibited widely, including in the Henie Onstad Kunstsenter and The Drawing Center, and participated in the Performa Biennial 11, Jerusalem Show IV, and the 1st Brooklyn Biennial. She is the co-founder of the Mutating Cities Institute and Associate Professor in the Humanities & Media Studies Department at the Pratt Institute.

Don Mee Choi is the author of *Hardly War* (Wave Books, 2016), *The Morning News Is Exciting* (Action Books, 2010), a chapbook, *Petite Manifesto* (Vagabond, 2014), and a pamphlet, *Freely Frayed* (Wave Pamphlet #9). She has received a Whiting Award, a Lannan Literary Fellowship, and the Lucien Stryk Translation Prize.

Gabrielle Civil is a black feminist performance artist, poet and translator originally from Detroit, Michigan. Over the last fifteen years, she has premiered over forty original solo and collaborative performance works around the world. Her translations have been published in *Two Lines*, *The Caribbean Writer*, *Dislocate* and the recent critical anthology *Amour, sexe, genre et trauma dans la Caraïbe francophone*. She is the author of *Swallow the Fish*, a memoir in performance art. The aim of her work is to open up space.

Teju Cole is a Nigerian-American author, most recently, of the essay collection *Known and Strange Things*. He is a photographer, a historian of art, and *The New York Times Magazine*'s photography critic.

Katrina Dodson is the translator from the Portuguese of Clarice Lispector's *Complete Stories*, winner of the 2016 PEN Translation Prize. She holds a PhD in Comparative Literature from the University of California, Berkeley with a dissertation on Elizabeth Bishop in Brazil. Her mother, half-sister and -brother, and other close relatives came to the U.S. from Vietnam as refugees in the 1970s. After focusing on Brazil in her work for over a decade, Katrina is looking for a way back to Vietnam.

Aja Couchois Duncan is a Bay Area educator, writer and coach of Ojibwe, French and Scottish descent. Her writing has been anthologized in *Biting the Error: Writers Explore Narrative* (Coach House Press), *Bay Poetics* (Faux Press), and *Love Shook My Heart 2* (Alyson Press). Her most recent book, *Restless Continent*, was published by Litmus Press and selected by Entropy Magazine as one of the best poetry collections of 2016. She holds an MFA in Creative Writing from San Francisco State University and a variety of other degrees and credentials to certify her as human. Great Spirit knew it all along.

Ashraf Fayadh is a Palestinian artist and poet born in Saudi Arabia in 1980. He attended college at Al-Azhar University in Gaza City in 2001, and has been active in the art scene in Saudi Arabia with organizations like Edge of Arabia, a British-Arabian art collaboration. Ashraf has also curated exhibitions of Saudi art during Jeddah Art week in Saudi Arabia and Europe at the 55th Venice Biennale. He is currently imprisoned in Saudi Arabia for apostasy, for the language in his poems.

Shahnaz Habib grew up in Kerala, India, and now lives in Brooklyn. Her writing has appeared in *Creative Nonfiction*, *Agni*, *Brevity*, *The Guardian*, *Elsewhere*, and other publications. She teaches writing at The New School and at Bay Path University.

Kyoko Hayashi is a celebrated Japanese author born in Nagasaki in 1930. After spending most of her childhood in Shanghai, in 1945 she returned to Nagasaki where she was mobilized to work full time in a munitions factory while still a student. Having lived through the atomic blast that destroyed the city on August 9, she eventually began to write, chronicling the stories of *hibakusha* (atomic bomb survivors). Hayashi first gained wide recognition in 1975 when her story "The Site of Rituals" (Matsuri no ba) won the prestigious Akutagawa Prize. Since that time, she has continued to write about the atomic bomb in her semi-autobiographical short stories and novels, receiving numerous awards. In 2005, the eight-volume *Kyoko Hayashi Complete Works* (*Hayashi Kyoko Zenshu*) was published in Japan, marking the sixtieth anniversary of the nuclear attacks.

Heraclitus was a pre-Socratic philosopher from Ephusus.

Hilda Hilst (1930–2004) was born in Jaú, a small town in the state of São Paulo, in 1930. a graduate of law from the University of São Paulo, she dedicated herself to literary creation from 1954 to her death. She is recognized as one of the most important and controversial names in Brazilian contemporary literature and received some of Brazil's most prestigious literary prizes.

Kim Hyesoon is one of the most prominent contemporary poets of South Korea. She lives in Seoul and teaches creative writing at the Seoul Institute of the Arts. Kim's poetry in translation includes *Mommy Must Be a Fountain of Feathers* (Action Books, 2008), *All the Garbage of the World, Unite!* (Action Books, 2011), *Sorrowtoothpaste Mirrorcream* (Action Books, 2014), *I'm OK, I'm Pig!* (Bloodaxe Books, 2014), and *Poor Love Machine* (Action Books, 2016).

Magda Kapa is a poet and photographer who was born in Greece and is now living in northern Germany, where she also teaches Modern Greek and English. Her first poetry collection, *All the Words*, was published by Phoenicia Publishing.

Mona Kareem is a poet and translator based in New York. She is the author of three poetry collections, some of which were translated into French, English, Spanish, Dutch, German, Farsi, Italian, and Kurdish. Mona is a doctoral candidate in the Comparative Literature program at Binghamton University. Her dissertation explores issues of subalternity in the Arab feminist novel. Her translation of Palestinian poet Ashraf Fayadh's collection *Instructions Within* was recently released from The Operating System press (Nov 2016) and has been long-listed for the 2017 Best Translated Book Award.

Madhu H. Kaza was born in Andhra Pradesh, India and works as a writer, educator, translator and artist in New York City. Her co-translation of a collection of short stories by the Telugu writer Volga was published in 2007 by Swecha Press. She is currently at work on her first novel, *Afterlife*.

John Keene's *Counternarratives* (New Directions) was published in the spring of 2015, with a British edition appearing in 2016. He is also the author of *Annotations* (New Directions), the poetry-art collection *Seismosis* (1913 Press), with artist Christopher Stackhouse, and the collaboration *GRIND* (ITI Press), with photographer Nicholas Muellner. His translation of Brazilian author Hilda Hilst's *Letters from a Seducer* appeared in 2014 from Nightboat Books and A Bolha Editora. A longtime member of the Dark Room Collective and a Graduate Fellow of Cave Canem, he currently is a member of the African Poetry Book Fund, and serves as Chair of African American and African Studies and Associate Professor of English at Rutgers University–Newark.

Rosamond S. King is a creative and critical writer, performer, and artist whose work is deeply informed by her cultures and communities, by history, and by a sense of play. Her poetry collection *Rock|Salt|Stone* will be published in early 2017 by Nightboat Books. Poems have appeared in more than two dozen journals and anthologies, including recent issues of *Drunken Boat*, *Harriet* (the Poetry Foundation's blog), *The North American Review*, and *The Cortland Review*, in addition to *The Caribbean Writer* and the award-winning *Kindergarde: Experimental Writing for Children.*

Wen Liu is a Taiwanese writer and scholar based in New York City. Her creative and academic works center on diasporic Asian queers' struggles of racialization, violence, and loneliness, but also the possibility for pleasure, solidarity, and new ways of belonging in the transnational urban queer space. She has published a poetry collection and a novel, *Diary of Collective Heartbreak* (Fembooks, 2012).

Bruna Dantas Lobato is a writer and literary translator from and to Portuguese. Her work has been published in *BOMB*, *Ploughshares* online, *The Christian Science Monitor*, *Words Without Borders*, *Asymptote* and elsewhere. She is originally from Natal, Brazil.

Orquídea Morales is a graduate student in American Culture at University of Michigan.

Lina Mounzer is a writer and translator living and working in Beirut. Her work has appeared in *Bidoun*, *Warscapes*, *The Berlin Quarterly*, *Chimurenga* and *Literary Hub*. She is the prose editor for the Beirut-based literary journal *Rusted Radishes*, and has translated, from Arabic to English, short stories by Chaza Charafeddine and Mazen Maarouf and a novel by Hassan Daoud. Among other things, she is at work on her first novel.

The Pakistani poet **Kishwar Naheed** has written ten volumes of poetry, two memoirs, travel narratives, collections of prose and criticism, edited anthologies and journals, collections of short stories for children, translations, and character-sketches; she also regularly contributes articles to the popular daily Urdu newspaper *Jang*.

Eiko Otake is a Japanese choreographer/dancer who has lived in New York since 1976. Since 1972 she and her partner Koma have collaborated as the performance team Eiko & Koma, creating and presenting a unique theater of movement in diverse venues worldwide, including numerous appearances at the American Dance Festival, the Brooklyn Academy of Music's Next Wave Festival, and a month-long "living" gallery installation at the Whitney Museum of American Art. Eiko & Koma have received many honors, including a MacArthur Fellowship in 1996.

Omar Pimienta is an interdisciplinary artist and writer who lives and works in the San Diego / Tijuana border region. He is currently in the University of California, San Diego's PhD program in Literature.

Mary Renda is a graduate student in Romance Languages and Literatures (Spanish) at the University of Michigan, Ann Arbor.

Eléna Rivera was born in Mexico City, and spent her formative years in Paris. She is the author of three books of poems, most recently *Scaffolding* from Princeton University Press (Princeton Series of Contemporary Poets, 2017), as well as numerous chapbooks. Her poetry has appeared in *The Nation*, *The New York Times*, *Denver Quarterly*, *Jacket2*, and *The Volta*, among other publications. She won the 2010 Robert Fagles prize for her translation of Bernard Noël's *The Rest of the Voyage* (Graywolf Press, 2011) and is a recipient of a 2010 National Endowment for the Arts Literature Fellowship in Translation.

Zohra Saed is a co-editor of *One Story, Thirty Stories: An Anthology of Contemporary Afghan American Literature* (University of Arkansas Press). Her essays on the Central Asian diaspora and their food history have appeared in *Eating Asian America: A Food Studies Reader* (NYU Press), and in *The Asian American Literary Review. Misspelled Cities/Falsch geschriebene Stadte: Sahar Muradi and Zohra Saed*, a bilingual English/German chapbook, was published for documenta13. She is the co-founder and editor of Brooklyn's Upset Press. As part of her work on Central Asian literatures she is translating Turkestani poems from the early twentieth century.

Mahwash Shoaib is a poet, translator and scholar. Her nonfiction, fiction, poetry and scholarly articles have appeared in many anthologies and journals. Her translations of the poetry of Kishwar Naheed, *Wrapped in Dread and Dynamite*, will be published by Upset Press. She currently teaches in Charlotte, North Carolina.

Eleni Stecopoulos was born in New York City and now lives in California. Her most recent book, *Visceral Poetics* (ON Contemporary Practice, 2016), explores languages and bodies, healing, translation, and diaspora, among other things.

Irene Stecopoulos was born on Kythera Island, Greece, and immigrated to New York City after World War II. She is a retired counselor and has been active in the American Association of University Women.

Cecilia Vicuña is a poet, visual artist and filmmaker born in Santiago de Chile. The author of twenty two books of poetry, she exhibits and performs internationally. In Chile, she founded the legendary Tribu No in 1967, a group that created anonymous poetic actions throughout the city. In 1974, exiled in London, she co-founded Artists for Democracy to oppose dictatorships in the Third World. She divides her time between Chile and New York.

Vimala is a poet, writer and an activist. Well known for the revolutionary and feminist perspective in her writings, she edited a Telugu political magazine, *Vimochana*, for ten years and edited a women's magazine *Stree Vimukti* in the 1990s. She has also served as a screenwriter for *Sakhi*, a program on ETV, a Telugu television channel. She has published numerous books and her works have been translated into Hindi and English. More than a dozen of her short stories have appeared in various magazines. Most recently, a collection of her short stories, *Few Stars and Some Tears*, was published in 2016.

Dagmawi Woubshet is an Associate Professor of English at Cornell University. He authored *The Calendar of Loss: Race, Sexuality, and Mourning in the Early Era of AIDS* (Johns Hopkins University Press, 2015), and co-edited *Ethiopia: Literature, Art, and Culture, a special issue of Callaloo* (2010). His work has appeared in various publications, including *Transition*, *Aperture*, and *African Lives: An Anthology*. He is currently working on three book projects: *Here Be Saints: James Baldwin's Late-Style*; *New Flower: A Memoir*; and the first English translation of Sebhat Gebre Egziabher's 1966 novel, *Säbatägnaw Mälak* (The Seventh Angel).

Permissions Acknowledgments

Rosamond S. King's "In Search of a Word" is included in her forthcoming book *Rock, Stone, Salt* (Nightboat Books, 2017).

Youmna Chlala's poems are excerpted from her forthcoming book *The Paper Camera* (Litmus Press, 2017).

A version of Zohra Saed's essay was published in *Langston Hughes: Poems, Photos and Notebooks from Turkestan* (Lost & Found, The CUNY Poetics Documents Initiative) 2015.

Mona Kareem's full-length translation of Ashraf Fayadh's *Instructions Within* was first published by the Operating System press in 2016.

Mahwash Shoaib's translation of Kishwar Naheed's "Horoscope" is from *Syah Hashiyeh mei Gulabi Rang / Pink in a Black boundary* (Lahore: Sang-e-Meel, 1986) and Kishwar Naheed's "Poem Standing on Fallujah's Door" is from *Wehshat aur Barood mei Lipti hui Shairi / Wrapped in Dread and Dynamite* (Lahore: Sang-e-Meel, 2009).

Eiko Otake's translation is excerpted from from her full-length translation of Kyoko Hayashi's *From Trinity to Trinity* (Station Hill

Press, 2010) and is reprinted with permission from Station Hill Press.

An extended version of "Epistles to the Dead" appears in Dagmawi Woubshet's *The Calendar of Loss* (Baltimore: Johns Hopkins University Press, 2015).

"Flicker and Flux: Versions of Heraclitus," translated by Magda Kapa and Teju Cole, was first published online on *Qarrtsiluni* (2011).

Don Mee Choi's essay "Darkness—Translation—Migration" was originally published on *Harriet*, the blog for the Poetry Foundation in April 2016.

John Keene's translation of "Tomfoolery" is excerpted from *Letters from a Seducer* by Hilda Hilst (Nightboat Books, 2014) and is reprinted with permission by Nightboat Books.

An earlier version of Aja Couchois "Duncan's Nomenclature, Miigaadiwin, a Forked Tongue" was published as a chapbook by CC Marimbo Press and most recently as part of a full collection titled *Restless Continent* by Litmus Press.

Lina Mounzer's essay, "War in Translation" was originally published online on *Lithub* (October 6, 2016).

Rosa Alcalá's translations of Cecilia Vicuna's poems are from Vicuna's first book, *Sabor a Mí* (1973). They will be published in *Cecilia Vicuña: New & Selected Poems (1966–2015)*, edited by Rosa Alcalá (Kelsey Street Press, forthcoming.)

Madhu H. Kaza and Sitaramayya Ari's translation of "The Dark Girl's Laughter" by Vimala was originally published online in *Waxwing* (February 2017).

Amy Sara Carroll's "The Desert Survival Series" is part of the Transborder Immigrant Tool, a project of the Electronic Disturbance Theater. The poems have been published in various places under a Creative Commons license.

Subscribe to Aster(ix)

www.ingramcontent.com/pod-product-compliance
Lightning Source LLC
Chambersburg PA
CBHW050403190726
48284CB00007BB/2416

* 9 7 8 1 9 4 2 5 4 7 0 6 8 *